NUMBERS

CW01638148

The Wiersbe BIBLE STUDY SERIES

Living a Life That Counts for God

David C Cook

transforming lives together

THE WIERSBE BIBLE STUDY SERIES: NUMBERS
Published by David C Cook
4050 Lee Vance View
Colorado Springs, CO 80918 U.S.A.

David C Cook Distribution Canada
55 Woodslee Avenue, Paris, Ontario, Canada N3L 3E5

David C Cook U.K., Kingsway Communications
Eastbourne, East Sussex BN23 6NT, England

The graphic circle C logo is a registered trademark of David C Cook.

LCCN 2013950191
ISBN 978-1-4347-0693-5
eISBN 978-1-4347-0747-5

The Team: Steve Parolini, Karen Lee-Thorp, Amy Konyndyk,
Nick Lee, Tonya Osterhouse, Karen Athen
Series Cover Design: John Hamilton Design
Cover Photo: iStockphoto

Printed in the United States of America
First Edition 2014

1 2 3 4 5 6 7 8 9 10

112813

Contents

Introduction to Numbers

The Importance of Being Counted

In different parts of the world, the word *count* shows up with assorted meanings. "Count us out!" is what American teenagers say when they have their own plans for the day. ("Include us out" is a variation of this phrase.) To a fight fan, "counted out" means that the boxer is on his back in the ring and has lost the fight.

But perhaps the most familiar use of the word *count* is as a synonym for dependability: "You can count on me!" It may have a military origin. Once soldiers are in position and have "counted off," they're ready to hear and obey their officer's orders. This is the way I'm using *count* in this book. To "be counted" means to be the kind of Christian God can depend on to get the job done right.

More Than Conquerors

The book of Numbers opens with a count of all the fighting men in the camp. They were "counted," but they couldn't be "counted on," so all but two of them died during Israel's march through the wilderness. Then the new generation was counted, and they were people whom the Lord could "count on." They trusted His Word, entered the Promised Land, and claimed it for their inheritance.

Studying the book of Numbers can help us better understand how God directs His people, why being faithful to Him is important, and how we can grow spiritually in the difficulties of life. We don't have to fail as did that first generation; we can be "more than conquerors through him who loved us" (Rom. 8:37).

—Warren W. Wiersbe

How to Use This Study

This study is designed for both individual and small-group use. We've divided it into eight lessons—each references one or more chapters in Warren W. Wiersbe's commentary *Be Counted* (second edition, David C Cook, 2010). While reading *Be Counted* is not a prerequisite for going through this study, the additional insights and background Wiersbe offers can greatly enhance your study experience.

The **Getting Started** questions at the beginning of each lesson offer you an opportunity to record your first thoughts and reactions to the study text. This is an important step in the study process as those "first impressions" often include clues about what it is your heart is longing to discover.

The bulk of the study is found in the **Going Deeper** questions. These dive into the Bible text and, along with helpful excerpts from Wiersbe's commentary, help you examine not only the original context and meaning of the verses but also modern application.

Looking Inward narrows the focus down to your personal story. These intimate questions can be a bit uncomfortable at times, but don't shy away from honesty here. This is where you are asked to stand before the mirror of God's Word and look closely at what you see. It's the place to take a good look at yourself in light of the lesson and search for ways in which you can grow in faith.

Going Forward is the place where you can commit to paper those things you want or need to do in order to better live out the discoveries you made in the Looking Inward section. Don't skip or skim through this. Take the time to really consider what practical steps you might take to move closer to Christ. Then share your thoughts with a trusted friend who can act as an encourager and accountability partner.

Finally, there is a brief **Seeking Help** section to close the lesson. This is a reminder for you to invite God into your spiritual-growth process. If you choose to write out a prayer in this section, come back to it as you work through the lesson and continue to seek the Holy Spirit's guidance as you discover God's will for your life.

Tips for Small Groups

A small group is a dynamic thing. One week it might seem like a group of close-knit friends. The next it might seem more like a group of uncomfortable strangers. A small-group leader's role is to read these subtle changes and adjust the tone of the discussion accordingly.

Small groups need to be safe places for people to talk openly. It is through shared wrestling with difficult life issues that some of the greatest personal growth is discovered. But in order for the group to feel safe, participants need to know it's okay *not* to share sometimes. Always invite honest disclosure, but never force someone to speak if he or she isn't comfortable doing so. (A savvy leader will follow up later with a group member who isn't comfortable sharing in a group setting to see if a one-on-one discussion is more appropriate.)

Have volunteers take turns reading excerpts from Scripture or from the commentary. The more each person is involved even in the mundane tasks, the more they'll feel comfortable opening up in more meaningful ways.

The leader should watch the clock and keep the discussion moving. Sometimes there may be more Going Deeper questions than your group can cover in your available time. If you've had a fruitful discussion, it's okay to move on without finishing everything. And if you think the group is getting bogged down on a question or has taken off on a tangent, you can simply say, "Let's go on to question 5." Be sure to save at least ten to fifteen minutes for the Going Forward questions.

Finally, soak your group meetings in prayer—before you begin, during as needed, and always at the end of your time together.

Order

(NUMBERS 1—4; 9:1–14)

Before you begin …

- *Pray for the Holy Spirit to reveal truth and wisdom as you go through this lesson.*
- *Read Numbers 1—4; 9:1–14. This lesson references chapter 1, "Order in the Camp," in* Be Counted. *It will be helpful for you to have your Bible and a copy of the commentary available as you work through this lesson.*

Getting Started

From the Commentary

The code name for the enterprise was "Operation Overlord." The more popular name was "D-Day"—June 6, 1943, when the combined Allied forces landed on Omaha Beach and signaled the beginning of the end of the war in Europe. It was the largest assembly of military personnel and matériel in the history of warfare. Historian Samuel Eliot Morison wrote, "The Allied forces of soldiers, sailors, aviators and supporting services amounted to 2.8 million men in England."

Moses was about to launch his own "Operation Overlord," and his greatest desire was that Jehovah, the Lord of Hosts, truly be Lord over the whole enterprise. More than two million Jews were anticipating entering Canaan, conquering the inhabitants, claiming the land, and enjoying their promised inheritance. But before all of this could happen, Moses had to organize this assembly of former slaves, who had been enjoying their freedom for only a year. It wasn't an easy task.

His preparation for conquest involved four stages: celebrating the Passover (9:1–14), numbering the soldiers (chap. 1), organizing the tribes (chap. 2), and assigning the priestly duties (chaps. 3—4).

—*Be Counted,* page 17

1. What was the purpose of each stage in Moses' preparation for conquest? (See From the Commentary.) Why was preparation so important to Moses? How did his preparation help? What were the biggest challenges Moses faced in this operation?

2. Choose one verse or phrase from Numbers 1—4; 9:1–14 that stands out to you. This could be something you're intrigued by, something that makes you uncomfortable, something that puzzles you, something that resonates with you, or just something you want to examine further. Write that here.

Going Deeper

From the Commentary

> The events recorded in Numbers 1—6 were preceded by those described in 7:1—9:15. We are now in the second year of Israel's national history (1:1; 9:1). The tabernacle was erected on the first day of the first month (Ex. 40:2, 17). The twelve tribal leaders began to bring their gifts on that day (Num. 7:1), a procedure that lasted twelve days (v. 78). On the thirteenth day, the Levites were consecrated (Num. 8), and on the fourteenth day, the Jews celebrated Passover (9:1–14).
>
> It was only fitting that the Israelites began their second year of freedom by commemorating the awesome night when God delivered them from Egyptian bondage, "A night of solemn observance to the LORD" (Ex. 12:42 NKJV). In looking back, the people would appreciate what God had

> done for them, and they could teach their children the significance of Israel's "independence day" (Ex. 12:26–28; 13:8–16). Unless parents remind their children of what the Lord has done, it won't be long before the next generation will drift from the faith (Deut. 6:1–9; see 2 Tim. 2:2).
>
> —*Be Counted*, page 18

3. Why was the celebration of the Passover so important for the traveling Israelites? How would that celebration have been particularly significant just a couple of years after the actual event? What does the Passover say to Christians today? (See John 1:29; 1 Cor. 5:7; Isa. 53:7; 1 Pet. 1:19; Rev. 5:6.)

More to Consider: According to Exodus 12, each family had to slay a lamb, roast it, and eat it with unleavened bread and bitter herbs (see Num. 9:11). The bread contained no yeast for two reasons, one practical and the other symbolic. The practical reason was that the Jews had to be ready to leave Egypt at any time, so they couldn't wait for the dough to rise. The symbolic reason involves the fact that, to a Jew, leaven represents evil, and the Jews were to be a pure people. All yeast had to be removed from their houses before Passover and be kept out during the week that followed. (See 1 Cor. 5:1–8; Matt. 16:6, 12; Gal. 5:9.) The bitter herbs reminded the Jews of their cruel bondage when they were slaves in Egypt. Why were these symbolic actions so important to the Jews? What are some of the symbolic actions Christians continue to recognize today? How can honoring the past through symbolic actions bring us closer to Christ?

From the Commentary

Anyone who was defiled had to be put out of the camp, because defilement has a way of spreading (Num. 5:1–2). This meant that these men were forbidden to participate in Passover. This new situation demanded new wisdom, so Moses turned to the Lord for help (James 1:5). Since it was the Lord's Passover, only the Lord could change the rules.

God's reply was gracious: Anyone who was defiled or absent from home during Passover the first month could celebrate the feast on the fourteenth day of the second month, but they had to be careful to follow the same divine instructions given in Exodus 12. God wasn't establishing a different Passover; He was only permitting His original Passover to be celebrated at a different time. None of the meat should be treated as common food (leftovers), and the lamb's bones must not be broken (see John 19:31–37).

This special consideration on the part of the Lord might lead some of the Israelites to start tampering with the divinely ordained Passover instructions, so God told Moses to warn them that the original rules were still in force, both for the first month and the second. Any Jews who were qualified to celebrate Passover the first month but didn't do so, hoping to do it more conveniently the second month, would be disciplined by God.

—*Be Counted*, page 19

4. God gave very specific instructions to His followers during this chapter in their history. Why do you think He chose to do this? What does this say about the relationship between God and His people? Is God's decision to offer a kind of grace to the defiled or absent a glimpse of the future of God's grace offered in Jesus? Why or why not?

From Today's World

In the days of Moses, rules and ritual played important roles in the daily lives of God's followers. Through Moses, the Israelites were given specific instruction for many aspects of daily life and were expected to practice specific rituals in honor of the God who was leading them. While Jesus' sacrifice changed the system of rules, introducing grace to our relationship with our Creator, rituals continue to play a part in most churches. The role rituals play varies dramatically from one church to the next, even within the same denomination.

5. How has the importance of ritual in our relationship with God changed since the time of Moses? What are the rituals in the church that matter most today? How do they bring people closer to God? How can they be misused or corrupted?

From the Commentary

The second month of the second year, thirteen months after the Exodus, Israel had to start preparing for battle. If Genesis is the book of beginnings and Exodus the book of redemption, then Numbers is the book of warfare. The Jews were in enemy territory, marching toward the land God would help them conquer, and they had to organize for confrontation and conflict. The phrase *able to go forth to war* is used fourteen times in this chapter. If God were to number the believers in the church today according to their ability to wage spiritual warfare, we wonder how big the army would be.

Some people are disturbed by the emphasis on warfare in certain parts of the Bible, and a few denominations have even removed from their hymnals militant songs like "Onward, Christian Soldiers." But their fears and criticisms are unfounded. "The LORD is a man of war" (Ex. 15:3) when it comes to punishing sin and removing evil. The nations that Israel destroyed in Canaan were living in abominable moral filth and sinning against a flood of light, and the Lord had been longsuffering with them (Gen. 15:13–16; Rom. 1:18ff.). Would anybody today criticize a surgeon for removing a cancerous life-threatening tumor from a patient's body?

—*Be Counted*, page 20

6. Why is the warring nature described in Numbers difficult for some believers to accept? What does this book teach us about God and His people during this time in history? Why would God choose violence to accomplish His will? Or was that God's choice? Explain.

From the Commentary

> Moses and Aaron were assisted in the census by the appointed leader of each tribe. These tribal leaders are also named in chapters 2, 7, and 10. It wasn't difficult to make the count because the nation was organized by households, families (clans), and tribes (Josh. 7:14), and there were rulers for each unit of ten, one hundred, and one thousand Israelites (Ex. 18:21). Note that Nahshon (Num. 1:7) was in the family tree of David (Ruth 4:20–22) and therefore an ancestor of Christ (Matt. 1:4).
>
> —*Be Counted*, pages 21–22

7. Why did each person have to prove his lineage as part of this numbering of soldiers? (See Num. 1:18.) Why was it so important that the Israelites be counted and vetted as God's people? What were the dangers of having

uncommitted people among the ranks of the Israelites? How could that have affected their success in battle?

From the Commentary

> Because of their important ministry as assistants to the priests, the Levites were exempted from military duty. The tabernacle was the most important structure in the entire camp, and only the priests and Levites could attend to it. Therefore, they weren't counted in the military census.
>
> One of the major themes of the book of Revelation is God's warfare against evil on earth and His receiving worship in heaven. Unless the people of God are right with the Lord in their worship, they can't face their enemies and defeat them in warfare. "Let the high praises of God be in their mouth, and a two-edged sword in their hand" (Ps. 149:6).
>
> —*Be Counted*, pages 22–23

8. How do worship and warfare interrelate in God's economy? How was that true in Moses' time? Is it still true today? Explain.

From the Commentary

> Whenever the camp moved, the ark of the covenant went before, carried by the priests. Then the tribes of Judah, Issachar, and Zebulun marched next, followed by the Gershonites and Merarites carrying the tabernacle proper (frames, curtains, coverings). Next came Reuben, Simeon, and Gad, followed by the Kohathites carrying the tabernacle furnishings. Ephraim, Manasseh, and Benjamin were next, while Dan, Asher, and Naphtali brought up the rear. The largest number of soldiers (186,400) led the way and the next largest (157,600) were the rear guard.
>
> The twelve tribes had to be careful not to camp too close to the tabernacle, for that area was reserved for the priests and Levites (Num. 2:2). To venture too near to the sacred tent could mean death (1:51).
>
> —*Be Counted*, page 24

9. Why was the tabernacle such a sacred place? What purpose did God have for choosing a specific place to represent His presence? What was the danger associated with being too close to the tabernacle (for those who weren't priests or Levites)? (See Num. 1:51; 2:2.)

More to Consider: Each tribe was to display its standard and each family its banner (1:52; 2:2). Nowhere in Scripture are we told the colors of these tribal banners or the emblems that were on them, and it's useless to conjecture. Jewish tradition suggests that the colors were those of the twelve gems in the high priest's breastplate (Ex. 28:15–29), but we can't be certain what some of those colors were. Jewish tradition also states that four of the tribal emblems came from Ezekiel 1:10 (and see Rev. 4:7) and assigned the lion to Judah (Gen. 49:9), the ox to Ephraim, the man to Reuben, and the eagle to Dan. What does this emphasis on family origin teach us about the Israelites? What are some ways the church similarly celebrates our heritage?

From the Commentary

Chapters 3 and 4 are devoted to the Levites, the men who served the Lord by assisting the priests in their ministry at the tabernacle. Moses records two numberings of the Levites, those one month old and older and those twenty years old and older, as well as the duties assigned to them. The Levites had no inheritance in the Promised Land but lived from a tithe of the gifts that the people brought to the Lord (Num. 18:20–24).

The priests were the descendants of Aaron, the first high priest, who had four sons: Nadab, Abihu, Eleazar, and Ithamar (Ex. 6:23). Nadab and Abihu brought unauthorized worship into the sanctuary and were killed by the Lord (Lev. 10). Eleazar was chief over the Levites (Num. 3:32) and eventually replaced his father as high priest

> (20:22–29). Ithamar had received the offerings for the building of the tabernacle (Ex. 38:21) and was in charge of the Gershonites and Merarites (Num. 4:28, 33). It was no insignificant thing to be one of God's priests, for the priests were God's anointed servants, especially consecrated for His glory (Ex. 28—29).
>
> God looked on Israel as His firstborn son (Ex. 4:22). He had spared Israel's firstborn at Passover but had slain the firstborn sons of Egypt (11:1–7; 12:29–30). For this reason, every firstborn male in Israel, whether human or animal, belonged to the Lord and had to be redeemed by a sacrifice (13:1–2, 11–13; 22:29–30; 34:19–20; Luke 2:7, 22–23).
>
> —*Be Counted*, page 25

10. In what ways was the nation of Israel meant to be a "kingdom of priests"? (See Ex. 19:5–6.) What role did the appointed priests have in helping to make this a reality? What role did the Levites play? In what ways are leaders and support teams today like the priests and Levites of old? In what ways are we all "priests"?

Looking Inward

Take a moment to reflect on all that you've explored thus far in this study of Numbers 1—4; 9:1–14. Review your notes and answers and think about how each of these things matters in your life today.

Tips for Small Groups: To get the most out of this section, form pairs or trios and have group members take turns answering these questions. Be honest and as open as you can in this discussion, but most of all, be encouraging and supportive of others. Be sensitive to those who are going through particularly difficult times and don't press for people to speak if they're uncomfortable doing so.

11. In Moses' day, God gave His people specific rules and commands. Does that sort of relationship with God appeal to you? Why or why not? What is it about a system of rules that can appear to be freeing?

12. What are some of the modern rituals in your church experience that resonate with you? What are rituals that don't resonate? How can you get more out of the rituals and traditions in your church life?

13. In what ways do you consider yourself a "priest" today? How does that term make you feel? What is it about the role of the priests in Moses' time that speaks to you? Does anything about their role trouble you?

Going Forward

14. Think of one or two things that you have learned that you'd like to work on in the coming week. Remember that this is all about quality, not quantity. It's better to work on one specific area of life and do it well than to work on many and do poorly (or to be so overwhelmed that you simply don't try).

Do you want to see how the value Moses placed on "order" might apply in your life? Be specific. Go back through Numbers 1—4; 9:1–14 and put a star next to the phrase or verse that is most encouraging to you. Consider memorizing this verse.

Real-Life Application Ideas: Moses and the leaders of the Israelites placed a high value on organization. As you consider the "battles" ahead of you in the coming weeks (work, family, community, etc.), how well organized are you to face them? Take some time to consider not only the practical concerns related to what's on your plate but also the spiritual dimension. Have you bathed the battles before you in prayer? Have you spent time in study about the issues surrounding those situations? Make a battle plan and stick to it.

Seeking Help

15. Write a prayer below (or simply pray one in silence), inviting God to work on your mind and heart in those areas you've noted in the Going Forward section. Be honest about your desires and fears.

Notes for Small Groups:

- *Look for ways to put into practice the things you wrote in the Going Forward section above. Talk with other group members about your ideas and commit to being accountable to one another.*
- *During the coming week, ask the Holy Spirit to continue to reveal truth to you from what you've read and studied.*
- *Before you start the next lesson, read Numbers 5—8; 9:15—10:10. For more in-depth lesson preparation, read chapters 2 and 3, "Dedication and Celebration—Part I" and "Dedication and Celebration—Part II," in* Be Counted.

Dedication

(NUMBERS 5—8; 9:15—10:10)

Before you begin ...

- *Pray for the Holy Spirit to reveal truth and wisdom as you go through this lesson.*
- *Read Numbers 5—8; 9:15—10:10. This lesson references chapters 2 and 3 in* Be Counted. *It will be helpful for you to have your Bible and a copy of the commentary available as you work through this lesson.*

Getting Started

From the Commentary

When Mohandas K. Gandhi was the spiritual leader of India, a missionary asked him what he thought was the biggest obstacle to Christian missions in India, and Gandhi replied, "Christians."

We may not like his answer, but we do have to face the fact that too often God's people get in the way of God's work. This is no better illustrated than in the book of

> Numbers where we see Israel repeatedly disobeying God and suffering for it. This explains why the Lord laid down some plain and practical rules for daily life in the camp of Israel. Israel was God's chosen people, separated from the other nations, and God wanted them to be different in the way they lived.
>
> —*Be Counted,* page 33

1. What kind of people did the Lord want the Israelites to be? How did the culture of the time affect their ability to be set apart? Why did the Israelites keep disobeying God?

More to Consider: God's glorious presence dwelt in the camp of Israel (Num. 5:3; Ex. 29:45); therefore, the camp had to be pure and holy in His sight. "I will walk among you and be your God, and you shall be My people," was His promise (Lev. 26:12 NKJV*), and with that gracious promise came the solemn responsibility: "Be holy, because I am holy" (Lev. 11:44–45).*

The concepts of "clean" and "unclean" were vital to daily life in Israel. In what ways was this more than just about personal hygiene? Why were unclean people put out of the camp until they had met the ceremonial requirements for reentry? Are there any parallels to this practice in our church today? Explain.

2. Choose one verse or phrase from Numbers 5—8; 9:15—10:10 that stands out to you. This could be something you're intrigued by, something that makes you uncomfortable, something that puzzles you, something that resonates with you, or just something you want to examine further. Write that here.

Going Deeper

From the Commentary

The word *defiled* is used nine times in Numbers 5, and three kinds of defilement are described.

(1) Physical defilement (vv. 1–4). Scholars aren't agreed on what leprosy was in ancient days, and some modern translations prefer "infectious skin disease." Whatever it was, leprosy was a dreaded disease that made the victims

ceremonially unclean. They had to live outside the camp, and if anybody approached them, they had to cry out, "Unclean, unclean!" (See Lev. 13.) If they were cured, they had to go through a lengthy process of cleansing before being admitted back into the camp (Lev. 14).

(2) Interpersonal defilement (vv. 5–10). The person who committed a trespass against another had to confess it and make restitution. (See Lev. 6:1–7; 7:1–10.) It wasn't enough just to confess the sin, say, "I'm sorry," and then bring a trespass offering to the priest. The offender had to pay the injured party (or a relative, or the priest) an amount of money equivalent to the loss incurred and add to it another 20 percent. In this way, the Lord taught His people that sin is costly and hurts people, and that true repentance demands honest restitution.

(3) Marital defilement (vv. 11–31). Faithfulness in marriage is a foundation stone for every society, for as goes the home, so goes the nation. In Israel, adultery not only defiled the people involved but also the land itself, and it was a sin detestable to God (Lev. 18:20, 24–29). Adultery was a capital offense. If proved guilty, both the adulterer and the adulteress were stoned to death (Deut. 22:22–24).

—*Be Counted*, pages 34–36

3. What do these passages reveal about God's desire for husbands and wives? What do they tell us about the consequences of unfaithfulness? How does adultery hurt more than just the wife and/or husband?

From the Commentary

> Don't confuse "Nazirite" with "Nazarene." Jesus was called a "Nazarene" because He came from Nazareth, a city despised by the people of Judea (John 1:43–46). The word *Nazirite* comes from a Hebrew word that means "to set apart, to dedicate." Jesus was not a Nazirite, because He touched dead bodies and drank the fruit of the vine, both of which were forbidden to Nazirites.
>
> Nazirites were Jewish men or women who dedicated themselves wholly to the Lord to fulfill the Nazirite vow of total separation. (In the KJV, the words *separate* and *separation* are used sixteen times in this chapter.) The Nazirite vow had both positive and negative aspects: Positively, it means being devoted to God; negatively, it meant abstaining from things God did not allow. Each Nazirite had a different goal in mind, but all of them wanted to glorify the Lord and obey His Word. They didn't isolate themselves from society, but rather were witnesses to others of the importance of total devotion to the Lord. Their vow was for a specified period (Acts 21:23–27) and a specified purpose.
>
> —*Be Counted*, pages 38–39

4. Review Numbers 6:1–8. What was the intent of total separation practiced by the Nazirite? Was it a realistic goal? What benefits did the Nazirites provide for the common man or woman? Is there an example of this Nazirite behavior in the church today? Explain.

From the Commentary

> Nobody but God can control the circumstances of life, and a Nazirite might accidentally be defiled. If that happened, he had to wait a week and on the seventh day shave his head. Since the period of dedication was suddenly over, and the hair was the sign of that dedication, the defiled hair had to go. However, the shorn hair wasn't made a part of the sacrifice as with the Nazirites who had completed their vows (v. 18).
>
> On the eighth day, the former Nazirite met the priest at the brazen altar and offered the required sacrifices: a bird for a sin offering, a second bird for a burnt offering, and a lamb for a trespass offering. This enabled the person to rededicate himself or herself to the Lord and make a new beginning. It was another opportunity to fulfill the vow made to the Lord.
>
> —*Be Counted*, page 39

5. What is the message inherent in the fact that Nazirites had a path back to their purpose after accidental defilement? What does this teach us about failure? How does this statement by Presbyterian pastor Alexander Whyte (1837–1921) speak to this very issue: "The victorious Christian life is a series of new beginnings"?

From the Commentary

On the first day of the first month, in the second year after Israel was delivered from Egypt, the tabernacle was erected and dedicated to the Lord (Ex. 40). On that day the twelve tribes of Israel began to bring special offerings to the Lord to be used by the priests and Levites in the tabernacle service. The people had donated generously to the building of the tabernacle (Ex. 25:1–8; 35:4—36:7), and now they were contributing to its ministry and maintenance.

A cursory reading of this long chapter (the longest in the Pentateuch) might give the impression that it contains nothing but repetition, for on twelve successive days each of the tribal leaders brought identical gifts. But we must not miss the point that God took notice of each gift, each leader, and each tribe on each successive day. In fact, each leader is mentioned twice, at the beginning of the report and at the end. We met these leaders in Numbers 1:5–16 and 2:3–32. The order is the same as that established for Israel whenever they marched to a new location.

While it's impossible by modern prices to calculate the value of these gifts, it's obvious that this was a very costly and generous offering. No doubt the twelve leaders got together and decided what to give, and then they gave their respective tribes opportunity to contribute. The gifts were both expensive and useful, showing generosity and practicality.

—*Be Counted*, page 42

6. Review Numbers 7:1–89. Why is such a long (and upon first glance, boring) passage included in Numbers? What does it reveal about the tribal leaders? What does it teach us about the importance of sacrifice? Of giving?

From the Commentary

> We are still examining the events that occurred in the camp of Israel at Mount Sinai on the day the tabernacle was erected and dedicated to God (Num. 7:1; Ex. 40:2, 17). It was the first day of the first month of the second year after Israel's exodus from Egypt.
>
> Everything that was done in the camp of Israel was ordered by the Lord. In the Holy Place of the tabernacle, before the veil, Moses would speak to God and God would speak to Moses from the mercy seat (Num. 7:89). Then Moses would pass along God's orders to the people of Israel. "So the LORD spoke to Moses face to face, as a man speaks to his friend" (Ex. 33:11 NKJV).
>
> Two things are involved here: divine revelation and divinely chosen leadership. All of God's people compose a holy priesthood (Ex. 19:6; 1 Peter 2:5, 9), but the Lord

has given spiritual leaders to His people (Eph. 4:11–16) and these leaders should be respected and obeyed (Num. 12:6–8; Heb. 13:7–9, 17). In the church today, God doesn't speak audibly to His people as He did to Moses, but as God's people worship together, pray, and study His Word, He reveals His will. "Prove all things; hold fast that which is good" (1 Thess. 5:21).

—*Be Counted*, page 47

7. What are the main themes of God's message to Moses in Numbers 8? Why was caring for the lamps important? What was the purpose of the dedication of the Levites? What expectations did God have as the nation marched into Canaan?

From the Commentary

The tabernacle was divided into two parts: the Holy of Holies, where God's glory rested above the mercy seat on the ark, and the Holy Place, which was separated from the Holy of Holies by the veil. There were three pieces of furniture in the Holy Place: the table for the twelve loaves

> of bread, the golden altar of incense before the veil, and the golden lampstand with its seven lamps.
>
> When the tabernacle was dedicated to the Lord, God's glory moved in (Ex. 40:34–35) and God's fire consumed the sacrifices on the altar (Lev. 9:23–24). But God didn't light the seven lamps on the golden lampstand in the Holy Place. This was the obligation of Aaron, the high priest, for he and his sons and their descendants would have the solemn responsibility of caring for the lampstand, trimming the wicks, adding the sacred oil, and making sure the light was shining. (See Ex. 25:31–40; 27:20–21; 37:17–24; Lev. 24:1–3.)
>
> —*Be Counted*, page 48

8. What did the lampstand signify? In what ways is the lampstand a symbol of Jesus Christ? (See John 8:12 and 1 John 1:5.) What does God's use of a lampstand reveal about God's character? About His grand plan for His people?

More to Consider: The lampstand was a reminder to the priests that Israel was called to be a light to the Gentile world (Isa. 42:6; 49:6). Unless the people obeyed God and worshipped Him as He commanded, Israel's light of witness would become dim and eventually go out. That's just what happened. Read Lamentations 4:13. Why did part of the blame for that lie with the priests? Whose responsibility is it today to keep the light from dimming?

From the Commentary

If Aaron and his sons were the "official clergy" in the camp, serving at the altar and in the tabernacle, then the Levites were the "dedicated laity," who assisted the priests in their ministry. They were taken "from among the children of Israel" (Num. 8:6, 14, 16, 19) as substitutes for the firstborn males who belonged to the Lord (vv. 16–18; see 3:40–51 and Ex. 13). The Levites belonged to the Lord (Num. 8:14), and He gave them to the priests as His special gift (v. 19). The Levites cared for the tabernacle, took the structure down for each march, carried it during the march, and then erected it again in the new location.

Since they were serving God at the tabernacle, the Levites had to be set apart for the Lord. First, they were cleansed by water (vv. 5–7), but unlike the priests, were merely sprinkled and not washed all over (Ex. 29:4). It is likely that Moses and Aaron sprinkled the 22,000 Levites (Num. 3:39) individually and not as a group. For further cleansing, the Levites were required to shave their bodies

> (see Lev. 14:8–9) and wash their clothes. (When consecrated to God, the priests were given special clothes to wear and weren't required to shave. See Ex. 29:5–9.)
>
> —*Be Counted*, page 50

9. Review Numbers 8:5–16. In what ways were the Levites presented to God as "living sacrifices"? (See Num. 8:8–14; Rom. 12:1.) In what ways are today's laity similar to the Levites of Moses' time? In practical terms, what does it mean to be a living sacrifice?

From the Commentary

> The Israelites were a pilgrim people, marching through the wilderness like an army, and they constantly needed the guidance of God. Their goal was the Promised Land, and the God who delivered them from Egypt promised to bring them into their inheritance if they would trust Him and obey His will.
>
> Knowing the will of God and doing it is vitally important to a fulfilled and fruitful Christian life. Jeremiah was correct when he said, "O Lord, I know the way of man is

> not in himself; it is not in man who walks to direct his own steps" (Jer. 10:23 NKJV). The child of God who fails to say, "If the Lord wills," is destined for disappointment and failure (James 4:13–17).
>
> —*Be Counted*, page 52

10. Why was knowing God's will so important to the Israelites in Moses' time? How did they discern God's will? (See Num. 9:15–23; 10:1–10.) How do we determine God's will today? (See Ps. 119:105; Acts 16:6–7; Rom. 8:26–34.)

Looking Inward

Take a moment to reflect on all that you've explored thus far in this study of Numbers 5—8; 9:15—10:10. Review your notes and answers and think about how each of these things matters in your life today.

Tips for Small Groups: To get the most out of this section, form pairs or trios and have group members take turns answering these questions. Be honest and as open as you can in this discussion, but most of all, be encouraging and supportive of others. Be sensitive to those who are going through particularly difficult times and don't press for people to speak if they're uncomfortable doing so.

11. What are some ways you separate yourself from temptations and bad influences? Is it easy to stay "clean" in a world that's unclean? What are the benefits of separating yourself from the world? What are the dangers?

12. God made a way for the Nazirites who were defiled to return to their roles. What are some of the ways you've been defiled in your own faith? What is God's path back to grace today? What are some of the failures God has used in your life to bring you closer to Him?

13. In what ways are you a light today? What are some of the things you do that reveal God to others? What are some of the things you do that tend to dim that light? What steps can you take to be more light than darkness?

Going Forward

14. Think of one or two things that you have learned that you'd like to work on in the coming week. Remember that this is all about quality, not quantity. It's better to work on one specific area of life and do it well than to work on many and do poorly (or to be so overwhelmed that you simply don't try).

Do you want to cleanse yourself in some area? Be specific. Go back through Numbers 5—8; 9:15—10:10 and put a star next to the phrase or verse that is most encouraging to you. Consider memorizing this verse.

Real-Life Application Ideas: This week, be a lampstand for God. Look for practical ways to shine God's light in all of your daily encounters. This could be anything from offering simple encouragement to someone who is struggling to buying lunch for a coworker "just because" to sharing the truth of the gospel in a conversation with a neighbor. Yes, the world is often a dark place, but this week you're to focus on the light you can bring to it, through Jesus.

Seeking Help

15. Write a prayer below (or simply pray one in silence), inviting God to work on your mind and heart in those areas you've noted in the Going Forward section. Be honest about your desires and fears.

Notes for Small Groups:

- *Look for ways to put into practice the things you wrote in the Going Forward section above. Talk with other group members about your ideas and commit to being accountable to one another.*
- *During the coming week, ask the Holy Spirit to continue to reveal truth to you from what you've read and studied.*
- *Before you start the next lesson, read Numbers 10:11—12:16. For more in-depth lesson preparation, read chapter 4, "Marching to Moab," in* Be Counted.

Marching

(NUMBERS 10:11—12:16)

Before you begin …

- *Pray for the Holy Spirit to reveal truth and wisdom as you go through this lesson.*
- *Read Numbers 10:11—12:16. This lesson references chapter 4 in* Be Counted. *It will be helpful for you to have your Bible and a copy of the commentary available as you work through this lesson.*

Getting Started

From the Commentary

The people of Israel camped at Mount Sinai about eleven months. They arrived there in the third month after their deliverance from Egypt (Ex. 19:1), and it was now the second month of the second year. During that time, God's law had been announced and the tabernacle had been constructed and dedicated. Moses had consecrated the

> priests and Levites, counted the soldiers, and organized the tribes. Israel was now a nation ready for action.
>
> —*Be Counted,* page 57

1. What was Israel's history like for the thirty-eight years after camping at Mount Sinai? (Skim Num. 10:11—22:1.) What were some of the nation's greatest failures during that time? What role did unbelief play in their very long journey?

More to Consider: The first ten chapters of Numbers record the activities of a nation obeying the Lord. "The Israelites did all this just as the Lord commanded Moses" (1:54). Read 2:34; 3:16, 51; 4:49; 5:4; 8:3, 20, 22; 9:5, 23. How is this theme repeated in these chapters? What happens in the chapters that follow 10? Why did the Israelites suddenly change from obeying God to disobeying Him?

2. Choose one verse or phrase from Numbers 10:11—12:16 that stands out to you. This could be something you're intrigued by, something that makes you uncomfortable, something that puzzles you, something that

resonates with you, or just something you want to examine further. Write that here.

Going Deeper

From the Commentary

> The cloud over the tabernacle moved, the priests blew the trumpets, the priests and Levites dismantled the tabernacle, and the people prepared to march. They had been comfortable while at Sinai, living in the same place for nearly a year and not having to face the rigors of a daily march. God's great victory over Egypt was fresh in their minds, and each morning when they gathered the manna, they were reminded of God's gracious provision for their every need.
>
> —*Be Counted*, page 58

3. Why did God provide manna for the Israelites? What might have tempted them to stay at Mount Sinai? What would the mood have been in the camp when God asked them to march? Consider the following statement: "The more comfortable we become, the less we welcome change, and yet there's

no growth without challenge and there's no challenge without change." How did this apply to the Israelites? How does it apply to us today?

From the Commentary

> Where each tribe marched in the procession wasn't an option; it was an obligation, an order from Almighty God. If the tribe of Dan or Asher grew tired of being at the end of the march and asked to take the lead, Moses would have refused their request, for the will of God in this matter wasn't negotiable. The people of Israel weren't on a pleasure trip, looking at the scenery. They were an army invading enemy territory and commanded by the Lord of Hosts. Each tribe was a division in the Lord's army (Num. 2:8; "division," NIV), and each division had to be in its proper place.
>
> —*Be Counted*, page 59

4. Why might God have given such specific instructions about the marching order? What lessons could He have been giving the Israelites in this? What happens when God gives us specific direction that we're unhappy about?

From Today's World

In Moses' time, the people were marching toward a very specific goal. But when they kept on marching after discovering the Promised Land, they didn't know where they were headed or how long they'd be marching. They had to trust their leaders during this time, which they did with varying degrees of success and failure. Today's church has a fairly simple mission: to preach the gospel and make disciples. Yet leaders are still called upon to head up the "marching orders" of the church, to lead the people where God wants them in literal and metaphorical ways. Many a church split has come when one group within the church believes God wants them to turn left, while another clearly hears God saying, "Go right."

5. What are some ways today's church is still marching in the wilderness? How can we know our leaders are taking us in the right direction? How ought we address the concerns we have when we think a leader is taking us in the "wrong" direction? How can trust and accountability help churches march in the right direction?

From the Commentary

> Bible students disagree over whether Moses was right or wrong when he asked Hobab to be Israel's "eyes" as they

> traveled in the wilderness. After all, wasn't the nation being led by the pillar of cloud and the ark of the Lord? And didn't God speak to Moses personally and reveal His will to him? Then why draft a human guide when they had so much help from heaven?
>
> But divine providence doesn't minimize or destroy human ability or responsibility. Israel didn't need Hobab to tell them where to march or where to camp; God would do that. But Hobab's knowledge of the land would assist them in making other decisions as they moved from place to place. Charles Spurgeon said: "We ought to learn from this, I think, that while we ever seek the guidance of God in providence, yet we may frequently find direction and guidance in the use of our own common sense, our own discretion with which the Lord has endowed us." We don't "lean on our own understanding" (Prov. 3:5–6 NIV), but neither do we ignore it. God wants us to act intelligently as well as believingly, and the spiritually minded Christian knows how to use both heart and mind in discerning God's will (Rom. 12:2).
>
> —*Be Counted*, page 60

6. Respond to the following statement: Divine providence doesn't minimize or destroy human ability or responsibility. How is this true for Moses? How is it true for us today? Why is it significant that Moses invited others to join Israel and enjoy God's blessings? What message does that give the church today?

From the Commentary

> The suggestion in 10:33–36 is that Moses and Aaron marched ahead of the tribes, just behind the ark. Each time the pillar of cloud signaled a move and the tribes were assembled, Moses prayed to God for guidance and victory, and when the nation stopped to camp, he prayed that God's presence would again rest with His people at the tabernacle. The ark would be put into the Holy of Holies and the pillar of fire would rest over the tent.
>
> No matter how many times the Israelites started and stopped in their journey, Moses repeated these prayers. He wanted the people to know that God, not Moses, was in charge of the nation, and that Israel was an army that depended on the Lord for victory.
>
> —*Be Counted*, pages 60–61

7. How are Moses' prayers like the invocation and benediction at a church worship service? In what ways were these brief prayers essential to Israel's well-being as a nation? How did Moses use these prayers to put God first in the life of the people?

From the Commentary

> So sinful is the human heart that it's prone to forget God's blessings, ignore God's promises, and find fault with God's providence. "Oh that men would praise the LORD for his goodness, and for his wonderful works to the children of men!" (Ps. 107:8, 15, 21, 31).
>
> In 11:1–3, history repeats itself. Three days after the great praise service by the Red Sea, the Jews complained against Moses and God because they didn't have water to drink (Ex. 15:22–27). Now, three days after leaving Sinai (Num. 10:33), the Jews complained again. It takes faith to be able to accept God's providential leading (Rom. 8:28), and Israel's faith wasn't very strong.
>
> Since the people had been camped in one location for nearly a year, perhaps the demands of the journey discouraged them, along with the monotony of the terrain. The NIV translates Numbers 11:1, "Now the people complained about their hardships."
>
> —*Be Counted*, page 61

8. Why did the Israelites complain so soon after God's great deliverance of them? What was the basis for their complaint? What does frequent complaining reveal about a person? How did God deal with the complainers? What does this teach us about God's relationship with His people during Moses' time?

More to Consider: Numbers 11:4–9 is the only place in the Old Testament where the Hebrew word asapsup *is used, and it describes a "rabble"—the "riffraff" that accompanied the Jews when they left Egypt (Ex. 12:38). Why might a group of "riffraff" have followed the Jews? (See Ex. 9:20.) What might they have been escaping? What was God's response to those who weren't sincerely following Him?*

From the Commentary

> The Lord had warned Israel that the way they treated the daily manna would be a test of their obedience to His word (Ex. 16:4; Deut. 8:3). By rejecting the manna, Israel really rejected the Lord (Num. 11:20 NIV), and it was this rebellious attitude that invited the judgment of God. This reminds us that the way we treat God's Word is the way we treat the Lord Himself.
>
> —*Be Counted*, page 65

9. In what ways is ignoring the Word, treating it carelessly, or willfully disobeying it like asking for the discipline of God? (See Heb. 12:5–11.) What are some healthy ways to cultivate an appetite for the holy Word of God? (See Job 23:12; Ps. 1:1; Jer. 15:16; Matt. 4:4; Luke 10:38–42; 1 Pet. 2:1–3.)

From the Commentary

People in places of spiritual leadership know that problems usually come in clusters of twos or threes. Why? Because Satan is alive and busy (1 Peter 5:8–9), and sinful human nature fights the holy will of God (Gal. 5:16–17). Just about the time the Lord helps you settle one crisis, another one appears.

Moses, Aaron, and Miriam were a team sent by God to help lead the nation of Israel (Mic. 6:4). God had used Miriam to save her younger brother's life (Ex. 2:1–10), and she was also a prophetess who led the Jewish women in praising God (15:20–21). Aaron was the elder brother in the family (7:7), appointed by God not only to assist Moses in confronting Pharaoh (4:10–17) but also to serve as the first high priest. Everybody in Israel knew that Moses, Aaron, and Miriam were God's chosen servants, but that Moses was the leader.

Three pieces of evidence lead to the conclusion that Miriam was the leader in this family rebellion: She is mentioned first in Numbers 12:1; the verb *spoke* is feminine in form, and Miriam alone was disciplined by the Lord. She didn't begin her assault by accusing Moses of usurping authority but by differing with him over his wife. (Most people who accuse God's servants rarely give the real reasons for their disagreements.) It's likely that Zipporah had died and Moses had taken a new wife and perhaps Miriam felt threatened by her. Also, when the

> Lord sent the Spirit upon the seventy elders, Miriam may have felt an erosion of her own authority.
>
> —*Be Counted*, page 66

10. Review Numbers 12:1–3. What was Miriam's complaint? Why did Aaron join her in this complaint? How did Moses respond to the complaint? In what ways is this circumstance similar to leadership challenges faced in the modern church?

Looking Inward

Take a moment to reflect on all that you've explored thus far in this study of Numbers 10:11—12:16. Review your notes and answers and think about how each of these things matters in your life today.

> *Tips for Small Groups: To get the most out of this section, form pairs or trios and have group members take turns answering these questions. Be honest and as open as you can in this discussion, but most of all, be encouraging and supportive of others. Be sensitive to those who are going through particularly difficult times and don't press for people to speak if they're uncomfortable doing so.*

11. Have you experienced seasons of disobedience toward God? What prompted those seasons? In what ways were you like the Israelites during these times? What brought you back to God?

12. Moses did his best to put God first as he led the Israelites. One way he did this was through frequent prayer. What are some of the ways you use prayer to put God first in your daily life? How can frequent and sincere prayer reveal God's will for your life? What are some of the things you've discovered about God's will through prayer times?

13. Have you ever felt like Miriam—that you deserved more authority than you were given? Describe that circumstance. What was the basis for your complaint? How was it resolved? What role does humility play in the life of good leaders? How is humility different from weakness?

Going Forward

14. Think of one or two things that you have learned that you'd like to work on in the coming week. Remember that this is all about quality, not quantity. It's better to work on one specific area of life and do it well than to work on many and do poorly (or to be so overwhelmed that you simply don't try).

Do you want to better trust God's direction for your life? Be specific. Go back through Numbers 10:11—12:16 and put a star next to the phrase or verse that is most encouraging to you. Consider memorizing this verse.

Real-Life Application Ideas: This section in Numbers is all about marching … and trust. This week, take a long walk with friends or family members with the sole purpose of listening to God as you walk. Choose a destination beforehand (but don't reveal it to your companions). Then encourage your fellow walkers to spend the walking time in prayer, inviting God's leadership and direction not only in the big decisions but the small ones as well. When you get to your destination, celebrate together God's goodness and faithfulness. (You might want to choose a fun ending destination—one with coffee or ice cream if your compatriots enjoy that sort of fellowship.)

Seeking Help

15. Write a prayer below (or simply pray one in silence), inviting God to work on your mind and heart in those areas you've noted in the Going Forward section. Be honest about your desires and fears.

Notes for Small Groups:

- *Look for ways to put into practice the things you wrote in the Going Forward section above. Talk with other group members about your ideas and commit to being accountable to one another.*
- *During the coming week, ask the Holy Spirit to continue to reveal truth to you from what you've read and studied.*
- *Before you start the next lesson, read Numbers 13—17. For more in-depth lesson preparation, read chapters 5, "Crisis at Kadesh," and 6, "A Question of Authority," in* Be Counted.

Crisis
(NUMBERS 13—17)

Before you begin ...

- *Pray for the Holy Spirit to reveal truth and wisdom as you go through this lesson.*
- *Read Numbers 13—17. This lesson references chapters 5 and 6 in* Be Counted. *It will be helpful for you to have your Bible and a copy of the commentary available as you work through this lesson.*

Getting Started

From the Commentary

At Kadesh-Barnea, on the border of Canaan, the people of Israel foolishly forfeited their opportunity to enter the Promised Land and claim their inheritance. This tragic failure has made the name *Kadesh* a synonym for defeat and lost opportunity. Israel's downfall at Kadesh is a reminder to us today that it's a dangerous thing to trifle with the will of God. You may end up spending the rest of your life wandering around, just waiting to die.

> In spite of what some of our hymns declare, Canaan is not a picture of heaven. Certainly there won't be any battles in heaven! Rather, Canaan is a picture of the inheritance God has planned for each of His children today, the work He wants us to do, and the places He wants us to occupy. Paul called it "good works, which God prepared beforehand that we should walk in them" (Eph. 2:10 NKJV). The Lord has a perfect plan for each of His children, but we can claim these blessings only by faith and obedience.
>
> —*Be Counted,* page 71

1. What are some of the ways we're like the people of Israel during this time in their history? What are some ways we walk by sight and not by faith? What do we miss out on when we walk by sight instead of faith?

2. Choose one verse or phrase from Numbers 13—17 that stands out to you. This could be something you're intrigued by, something that makes you uncomfortable, something that puzzles you, something that resonates with you, or just something you want to examine further. Write that here.

Going Deeper

From the Commentary

> God delivered His people from Egypt that they might enter the Promised Land and enjoy the blessings prepared for them. Forty years later, Moses reminded the new generation, "And he brought us out from there [Egypt], that he might bring us in, to give us the land which he swore unto our fathers" (Deut. 6:23; see Ezek. 20:6). The Lord had promised the land to the descendants of Abraham, Isaac, and Jacob (Gen. 12:7; 13:15; 17:8; 28:13; 35:12) and had reaffirmed that promise through Moses (Ex. 3:8, 17; 6:4, 8; 13:5; 33:3).
>
> —*Be Counted*, page 72

3. In what ways had the Israelites begun to walk by sight and not faith? How did God remind the people of His faithfulness and His promise? Why did they have trouble accepting this? Why is doubt such a common theme throughout Scripture?

More to Consider: The twelve spies chosen were different men from the leaders named in Numbers 1—2, 7, and 10. These spies had to be younger men who could endure the rigors and dangers involved in reconnoitering the land. We meet Caleb for the first time in 13:6, but he'll be mentioned thirty-one more times in the Old Testament. Why does he get such a prominent place in Old Testament history? What did he (and Joshua) do that the other spies did not? What does this teach us about how God rewards those who trust Him?

From the Commentary

> The twelve spies traveled about five hundred miles during the forty days of their survey of Canaan, but they discovered nothing that God hadn't already told them! They already knew the names of the pagan nations that lived in the land (Gen. 15:18–21), that it was a good land (Ex. 3:8), and a rich land flowing with milk and honey (vv. 8, 17). They saw the incredible fruit of the land and brought back a huge bunch of grapes for the people to see. They even visited Hebron, where the patriarchs of Israel were buried with their wives (Num. 13:22; Gen. 23:2, 19; 49:29–31; 50:13). Did the reminder of the faith of Abraham, Isaac, Jacob, and Joseph encourage their own trust in God? For ten of the spies, the answer is no.
>
> —*Be Counted*, page 73

4. In what ways was the survey of the land a good idea militarily? How did this approach fall short spiritually? What had God promised the Israelites? Why did they struggle to trust this promise?

From the Commentary

Someone has defined a committee as "a group of people who individually can do nothing and collectively decide nothing can be done." Because they lacked faith, all the spies except Caleb and Joshua were discouraged at the prospect of entering the land and fighting the enemy, and their discouragement quickly spread throughout the camp. Doubt had turned into unbelief, and unbelief is rebellion against God (Num. 14:9; Heb. 3:16–19).

It's interesting how the ten spies identified Canaan as "the land to which you sent us" (Num. 13:27 NIV) and "the land through which we have gone" (v. 32 NKJV), but not as "the land the Lord our God is giving us." Because these ten men were walking by sight, they didn't really believe God's promises. They looked at the people of the land and saw giants; they looked at the Canaanite cities and saw high walls and locked gates; and they looked at

> themselves and saw grasshoppers. If only they had looked by faith to God, they would have seen the One who was able to conquer every enemy and who sees the nations of the world as grasshoppers (Isa. 40:22). "We are not able" is the cry of unbelief (Num. 13:31 NKJV), but, "Our God is able" is the affirmation of faith (Dan. 3:17; see Phil. 4:13).
>
> —*Be Counted*, page 74

5. Read Numbers 13:26–33 and Deuteronomy 1:26–28. Why did the ten spies see only danger and trouble in the land? How does the following statement relate to their circumstance: "A faith that can't be tested can't be trusted." How is this true for believers today? Why does God test our faith? (See 1 Pet. 1:1–9.)

From the Commentary

> In the camp of Israel, unbelief and discouragement spread rapidly from heart to heart, and before long "all the congregation lifted up their voice, and cried; and the people wept that night" (Num. 14:1, and note vv. 2 and 10).

> The next day, the whole congregation criticized Moses and Aaron and lamented the fact that the nation hadn't perished in Egypt or in the wilderness. When your eyes are on yourself and your circumstances, you lose your perspective and say and do ridiculous things.
>
> However, the Jews had a long record of complaining against the Lord and their leaders, and being judged for it. Their murmuring began on the night of the exodus when they were sure Pharaoh's army was going to kill them (Ex. 14:10–14). As Israel entered the wilderness of Shur, they complained because they didn't have water to drink (15:22–27), and then they murmured because they missed the delicious meals that were provided in Egypt (Ex. 16). "Would that we had died in the land of Egypt!" was their favorite lament. At Rephidim, the people were ready to stone Moses because they had no water (17:1–7), and at Taberah some of the people complained and were killed by fire (Num. 11:1–3). Shortly after that, the mixed multitude incited the Jews to ask for meat to eat, and Moses became so discouraged he wanted to die (v. 4ff.).
>
> —*Be Counted*, pages 75–76

6. Review Numbers 14:1–10. In what ways was the response of the Israelites to the spies' reports like the way congregations today sometimes respond to discouraging news? Why don't hope and possibility spread as quickly as despair and disappointment? How does trust in God help us to embrace hope rather than despair?

From the Commentary

More than once, Israel in her pride tempted God in the wilderness, and He responded with judgment (Deut. 6:16; Ps. 78:17–18, 41, 56; 95:8–11; 106). Like a stubborn child, the Jews never seemed to learn their lesson. Instead of pleasing the Lord, who had done so much for them, they provoked Him to anger and dared Him to act.

As he had done when Israel worshipped the golden calf (Ex. 32), Moses interceded for the people (see 14:11–19) and turned away the wrath of God. For a second time, God offered to make a new nation out of Moses and completely destroy the Jewish people (Num. 14:11–12), but Moses refused. It's the mark of great and godly leaders that they think only of the good of their people and not their own personal gain. In fact, Moses was willing to die for the nation rather than let God destroy it (Ex. 32:32; see Rom. 9:1–3).

Moses reasoned with God and argued first of all that His glory would be tarnished if Israel were destroyed. The nations had heard what God did in Egypt, but they would no longer fear Him if Israel were destroyed. The nations would say, "He brought Israel out of Egypt but wasn't able to bring them into the land. This means that the gods of the land of Canaan are stronger than Jehovah!" The great concern of Moses was that God be glorified before the nations.

His second argument was the covenant God had made with the patriarchs years before. The Lord had promised Abraham, Isaac, and Jacob that He would give them the

> land, and He could not go back on His word (Gen. 13:17; 15:7–21; 28:13; 35:12).
>
> For his third argument, Moses pointed to the character of God and quoted what God Himself had declared to him on Mount Sinai (Num. 14:17–18; Ex. 34:6–7).
>
> —*Be Counted*, pages 77–78

7. Did Moses change God's mind about the wayward Jews? Why or why not? What lessons does God teach through His encounters with Moses about the people of Israel? How did God ultimately solve the dilemma of the sinful nation? (See Rom. 3:21–31.)

From the Commentary

> The events described in Numbers 15—17 probably occurred shortly after Israel's tragic failure at Kadesh-Barnea, and they reveal clearly that the people still hadn't learned how to trust and obey. No wonder the Lord rejected the older generation and made a new beginning with the younger generation!

God had a special word of encouragement for the younger generation: "After you enter the land I am giving you as a home" (Num. 15:2 NIV). The younger generation faced thirty-eight years of wandering, but the Lord guaranteed that they would one day enter the land and claim their inheritance. The children suffered because of the sins of their fathers and had to participate in history's longest funeral march.

The older generation of Israelites repeatedly refused to submit to the authority of God's Word as well as the authority of God's appointed leaders. Believers today commit the same sins, and the consequences are evident: divided churches, dysfunctional families, and disobedient individuals who wander from church to church but never accomplish much for the Lord.

—*Be Counted*, page 84

8. The younger generation was promised a great reward, but still they had to wander for nearly forty years. What does this reveal about God's timing? About God's promises? What role does submission to God's Word and leaders play in a believer's life? (See Heb. 13:7–9, 17 and Eph. 2:10.) How does submission to God's will help us to accomplish His purpose?

More to Consider: The phrase to make "an aroma pleasing to the Lord" is found five times in Numbers 15:1–21 (15:3, 7, 10, 13–14). The five basic Mosaic offerings were the burnt offering, meal offering, peace offering, sin offering, and trespass offering (Lev. 1—7). The first three were "sweet savor" sacrifices, designed to please the Lord, but the sin offering and the trespass offering were not "sweet savor" because they dealt with guilt and sin, and there's nothing pleasing to God about sin.

How did the burnt offering typify the worshipper's devotion to God? How did the meal (grain) offering speak of the worshipper's dedication of his labor to the Lord? What did the peace (trespass) offering represent? What are the different kinds of offerings we give to God in today's church?

From the Commentary

The sacrifices described in Leviticus 1—7 took care of sins of commission, but the instructions in 15:22–29 have to do with unintentional sins of omission, things that the people should have done but didn't do. The sin might be corporate and involve the entire nation (Num. 15:24–26), or it might be the transgression of an individual (vv. 27–29). Even though the people who sinned didn't realize their failure, what they didn't do was still a sin and had to be dealt with. "I didn't know" will not avail at the throne of God.

The sinners had to come God's appointed way so He could forgive them and restore them to fellowship and blessing. If the whole nation sinned, they had to bring a young bull

> for a burnt offering (dedication), plus the required drink offering and grain offering, and a male goat for a sin offering (atonement). The individual who sinned had to bring a year-old female goat as a sin offering. God promised to forgive those who truly sought Him by faith (vv. 25–26, 28). Of course, forgiveness didn't come because of the blood of animals, but because Christ shed His blood for sinners, fulfilling what these animals symbolized (Heb. 10:1–18).
>
> —*Be Counted*, page 88

9. Sometimes we sin against the Lord by what we do, and sometimes by what we don't do (Luke 7:36–50). What are some of the "sins of omission" the Israelites committed? What are some common ones people commit today? How do we recognize sins of omission?

From the Commentary

> When you review the history of Israel, from Egypt to Canaan, you discover that the nation got into trouble every time they resisted the leadership of Moses and Aaron. Whenever God sought to build the people's faith

> by bringing them into a difficult situation, they immediately rebelled against Moses and Aaron, blamed them for their plight, and made plans to return to Egypt.
>
> Chapters 16 and 17 record two challenges to the leadership of Moses and Aaron, one from a group of Levites (Num. 16:1–35) and one from the people as a whole (vv. 41–50). Out of each of these confrontations came a visible reminder to the Jews of their rebellion: the brass covering on the altar (vv. 36–40) and Aaron's rod that budded (17:1–13).
>
> —*Be Counted*, page 90

10. What were the two challenges to the leadership of Moses and Aaron? (See Num. 16:1–35 and 16:41—17:13.) Why did the Israelites repeatedly struggle to obey God? (See Deut. 31:16–30.) Why do Christians today often struggle to obey God?

Looking Inward

Take a moment to reflect on all that you've explored thus far in this study of Numbers 13—17. Review your notes and answers and think about how each of these things matters in your life today.

Tips for Small Groups: To get the most out of this section, form pairs or trios and have group members take turns answering these questions. Be honest and as open as you can in this discussion, but most of all, be encouraging and supportive of others. Be sensitive to those who are going through particularly difficult times and don't press for people to speak if they're uncomfortable doing so.

11. How does doubt influence your relationship with God? Where does that doubt come from? What are some practical things you can do to turn from doubt to trust?

12. What are some ways your faith has been tested? What did you learn from those situations? Have you grown closer to God through testing? If so, how?

13. What are some of the sins of omission you've struggled with in the past? How do sins of omission often lead to guilt? How do you deal with the things you didn't do but should have? Where and when does God's grace appear when you've committed a sin of omission?

Going Forward

14. Think of one or two things that you have learned that you'd like to work on in the coming week. Remember that this is all about quality, not quantity. It's better to work on one specific area of life and do it well than to work on many and do poorly (or to be so overwhelmed that you simply don't try).

Do you want to confess and address a sin of omission? Be specific. Go back through Numbers 13—17 and put a star next to the phrase or verse that is most encouraging to you. Consider memorizing this verse.

Real-Life Application Ideas: Discernment is a key component in our ability to follow God. This week, practice discernment for upcoming decisions in your life. Seek God's truth through prayer, Scripture reading, and the wise counsel of friends and leaders. Discernment isn't something that comes without practice and patience. Welcome both as you seek God's will.

Seeking Help

15. Write a prayer below (or simply pray one in silence), inviting God to work on your mind and heart in those areas you've noted in the Going Forward section. Be honest about your desires and fears.

Notes for Small Groups:

- *Look for ways to put into practice the things you wrote in the Going Forward section. Talk with other group members about your ideas and commit to being accountable to one another.*
- *During the coming week, ask the Holy Spirit to continue to reveal truth to you from what you've read and studied.*
- *Before you start the next lesson, read Numbers 18—21. For more in-depth lesson preparation, read chapters 7, "Another Crisis at Kadesh," and 8, "Marching in Victory—and Defeat," in* Be Counted.

Victory and Defeat

(NUMBERS 18—21)

Before you begin …

- *Pray for the Holy Spirit to reveal truth and wisdom as you go through this lesson.*
- *Read Numbers 18—21. This lesson references chapters 7 and 8 in* Be Counted. *It will be helpful for you to have your Bible and a copy of the commentary available as you work through this lesson.*

Getting Started

From the Commentary

It's probable that the instructions in chapters 18 and 19 were given by the Lord while Israel was still at Kadesh-Barnea. However, when you get to chapter 20, the nation has completed its thirty-eight years of wandering and is back at Kadesh (Num. 20:1, 16).

Very little is written in Numbers about Israel's years of wandering, although a list of their camping places is

> found in Numbers 33. Miriam died in the first month of the fortieth year (20:1), when the nation had returned to Kadesh, and Aaron died in the fifth month of that same year (33:38). When Moses died at the end of the fortieth year (Deut. 1:3), the entire older generation had perished, except for Joshua and Caleb, who were permitted to enter Canaan.
>
> —*Be Counted,* page 99

1. What was God's response to the people's stubbornness about trusting Him? How did God still show care and love for His people, despite their disobedience? Why did He do this? (See Ps. 106:8.) What does this say about Him?

2. Choose one verse or phrase from Numbers 18—21 that stands out to you. This could be something you're intrigued by, something that makes you uncomfortable, something that puzzles you, something that resonates with you, or just something you want to examine further. Write that here.

Going Deeper

From the Commentary

Because of the Lord's judgments against the rebels at the tabernacle (Num. 16:31–35) and His miraculous defense of Aaron's high priestly ministry (17:10–13), the people of Israel were terrified even to have the tabernacle in their camp. "Are we all going to die?" they cried (v. 13 NIV). Actually, God's presence in their camp was the distinctive mark of the people of Israel (Ex. 33:1–16), for Israel was the only nation to have the glory of the living God present with them and going before them.

God spoke expressly to Aaron (Num. 18:1, 8, 20) and thereby elevated his high priestly ministry even more. The Lord made it clear that it was the responsibility of the priests to minister in the tabernacle and protect it from defilement, and it was the responsibility of the Levites to assist the priests in their tabernacle ministry. As long as the priests and Levites obeyed this rule, there would be no judgment sent to the people (v. 5).

The priestly ministry was a serious matter, for if the priests didn't follow God's instructions, they might die. If they permitted an unauthorized person to come near the tabernacle or to minister there, God could slay them. It was dangerous to disobey even in the matter of how they dressed (Ex. 28:35, 42–43) or if they washed regularly (30:17–21). God held Aaron and his sons responsible for offenses committed against the sanctuary and the priesthood.

—*Be Counted*, page 100

3. Review Numbers 18:1–7. In what ways was the priesthood God's gift to Israel? How were the Levites God's gift to the priests? What does this entire section teach us about the crucial role of leadership?

More to Consider: God doesn't dwell in temples made with hands (Acts 7:48), but He does dwell in our bodies by His Holy Spirit (1 Cor. 6:19–20) and among His people in the local assembly (3:16–17). What does this suggest about how we should treat our bodies? What does it mean that assemblies of believers are a "sacred temple" for God?

From the Commentary

> As servants of God, the priests and Levites deserved to be cared for by the people of God. Unlike the other tribes, Levi would have no inheritance in the Promised Land, for the Lord was their inheritance (Num. 18:20; Deut. 10:8–9; Josh. 13:14, 33; 14:13; 18:7), and the Levites would be given forty-eight towns to live in (Num. 35:1–8; Josh. 21). Both the priests and Levites were cared for by means of the sacrifices, offerings, and tithes of the people.

God assigned to the priests portions of the meal offerings, sin offerings, trespass offerings, and peace offerings (Lev. 6:14—7:38), as well as the firstfruits (Deut. 26:1–11) and the firstborn animals that the people brought to the Lord. Some of this food only the priests could eat, but much of it could be shared with their families. However, whoever in the priestly family ate of the sacrifices given to God had to be ceremonially clean and treat the food with reverence, because it had been sanctified by being presented to God.

The Levites were given the tithes, which the people brought to God's sanctuary, for 10 percent of the produce belonged to the Lord. The Jews were obligated to pay three different tithes: a tithe to the Levites (Num. 18:21–24), a tithe "eaten before the LORD" (Deut. 14:22–27), and a tithe every three years that was given to the poor. The Levites in turn were to take a tithe of what they received, offer it to the Lord, and give it to the high priest.

—*Be Counted*, page 101

4. What is the main principle being offered in this section? Why is it important to support our leaders and teachers? How does God help us to be able to do just that?

From the Commentary

> God expected the Levites to tithe what they received and share it with the high priest (Num. 18:25–32). On occasion I've met people in Christian service who don't give to the Lord's work because they consider themselves exempt. "We're serving the Lord and all that we have belongs to Him," they argue, but their argument doesn't hold water. The Levites were serving God full time, yet they tithed what they received.
>
> —*Be Counted*, page 102

5. What was the purpose of tithing in the time of Aaron? What was the purpose of Abraham's and Jacob's tithing before the law was given? (See Gen. 14:20; 28:22.) What does 2 Corinthians 8—9 add to the conversation about tithing? What should be our motivation to give?

From the Commentary

> In their daily lives, the Jewish people had to be sensitive to what was "clean" and what was "unclean," for this

> determined their relationship to the Lord and the other people in the camp. God's rule was, "You shall be holy for I am holy," a statement found eight times in the Bible (Lev. 11:44–45; 19:2; 20:7, 26; 21:8; 1 Peter 1:15–16). The regulations about "clean and unclean" are spelled out in detail in Leviticus 11—15, telling the Israelites what they could eat, how they should deal with bodily discharges and infections, and what to do about dead bodies.
>
> —*Be Counted*, page 102–103

6. Certainly there was a hygienic purpose behind the laws of cleanness, but what was the spiritual purpose? How does a message encouraging cleanness also encourage healthy spiritual practices? What are the dangers of emphasizing the rules over the intent?

From the Commentary

> The death of Miriam must have affected Moses and Aaron deeply. It was Miriam whom the Lord used to save Moses' life when he was a baby, and she even arranged for their own mother to raise Moses and be paid for it (Ex. 2). She

had led the praises of the women at the Red Sea (Ex. 15) and had endured the wilderness trials with her brothers. The only blemish on the record is her criticism of Moses (Num. 12), but is there any servant of God who has a spotless page?

It was a conditioned reflex: Whenever the Israelites faced a difficulty, they complained about it to Moses and Aaron and wept because they hadn't stayed in Egypt. Difficulties bring out either the best in people or the worst; difficulties either mature us or make us more childish (James 1:2–8). Israel's words and attitudes revealed clearly that their hearts were still in Egypt. What a picture of the professed Christian who still loves the world (1 John 2:15–17) and turns to the world for help whenever there's a problem!

It was the people who should have been on their faces, confessing their sins and seeking God's forgiveness, but once again, Moses and Aaron fell before the Lord and sought His wisdom and help (Num. 14:5; 16:4, 22, 45; 22:31). Spiritual leaders pay a price as they seek to serve God's people, but the people usually don't appreciate it. The same people repeat the same sins and refuse to trust God and obey Him.

The rod was the same one Moses had used to do wonders in Egypt, especially to open the Red Sea. The Hebrew word for "rock" means a high cliff, a place for a fortress, and not a boulder. God is able to solve our problems no matter what the circumstances are, provided we trust Him and do His will.

Provoked in his spirit, instead of speaking to the rock, Moses smote it twice. He also spoke angrily to the people, calling them "rebels," and he gave the impression that he and Aaron had supplied the water. It was a sad demonstration of hostility by the meekest man on the earth (Num. 12:3), showing that we can fail in our strengths as well as our weaknesses.

—*Be Counted*, pages 105–106

7. Review Numbers 20:1–13. How does this story reveal Moses' human nature? How might weariness have influenced the way he responded here? What does Psalm 106:32–33 tell us about Moses' anger? How did striking the rock ruin a picture of the Messiah, who gives living water to His people? (See Ex. 17:1–7; John 7:37–39.) What does it say about God that He gave the water, even though Moses' attitudes and actions were all wrong?

From the Commentary

Both Moses and Aaron had rebelled against God when Moses smote the rock, so neither of them would enter the Promised Land. On the first day of the fifth month of that fortieth year (Num. 33:38), Moses, Aaron, and Eleazar went somewhere on Mount Hor because it was now time for Aaron to die. Moses would say good-bye to a beloved brother and Eleazar to a revered father. Aaron was 123 years old (33:38–39).

However, Aaron's death didn't interrupt the ministry of the priesthood, for Eleazar took his place. As John Wesley used to say, "God buries His workmen but His work goes on." In fulfillment of the law (Ex. 29:29–30), Moses took the holy garments from his brother, Aaron, and put them on Eleazar. He probably anointed him as well for the new office. When Moses and Eleazar returned to the camp without Aaron, and the people saw Eleazar dressed in the robes of the high priest, they knew that Aaron's life had ended. They mourned for Aaron for thirty days, which takes us now into the sixth month.

Eleazar was the third son of Aaron (Num. 3:2); the first two, Nadab and Abihu, were slain by the Lord for defiling the tabernacle with false fire (Lev. 10). Before becoming high priest, he was the chief leader of the Levites for caring for the tabernacle (Num. 3:32; 4:16). He would assist Moses in taking the census of the new generation (26:1–3) as well as in commissioning Joshua to succeed Moses (27:18–23). When Israel had conquered the land, Eleazar helped Joshua assign each tribe its inheritance (34:17; Josh. 14:1; 19:51).

—*Be Counted*, pages 108–109

8. What did Moses do after his personal failure? What message does he give us through his action of getting right back to work? How can we learn from his failure to better deal with the same in our own spiritual lives?

From the Commentary

Life goes on. The Jews completed their mourning for Aaron and were soon back on the road and back in the battle. Arad was a Canaanite town about twenty miles south of Hebron, so the new generation of Israelites was facing its first conflict with the Canaanites. The Jewish army would spend at least seven years conquering the nations in the Promised Land, so God gave them some military training as they marched on the road to Atharim.

The news of Israel's march from Egypt to Kadesh had gone before them and the rulers of the city-states in and around Canaan weren't going to give in to these intruders without a fight. Apparently Israel wasn't prepared for this first attack because some of their people were taken prisoners, but the leaders immediately turned to the Lord for His help. They vowed to utterly destroy the Canaanites and their cities if the Lord would give them victory.

> To "utterly destroy" meant to devote something completely to the Lord (Lev. 27:28–29; Deut. 7:2–6), wiping out the people and their cities and giving all the spoils to God. This is what Israel would do at Jericho (Josh. 6:17–21), and because Achan took what belonged to God, he was slain (Josh. 7). The Canaanite culture was unspeakably wicked, especially their religious practices, and God wanted these nations removed from the earth.
>
> God gave Israel victory over the enemy and the people kept their promise. They destroyed Arad and the other cities connected with it and gave a new name to the area: Hormah, which means "destruction."
>
> —*Be Counted*, pages 113–114

9. How was this conflict different from the battle Israel experienced thirty-eight years before when they tried to engage the enemy without God's blessing? (See Num. 14:39–45.) What lesson did the Israelites learn from the first battle? From the one described in this section?

More to Consider: A bountiful supply of manna had been sent from heaven each morning since shortly after the exodus (Ex. 16:1–22), so for forty years, God had been feeding His people the nourishment they needed. Manna was "angels' food" (Ps. 78:25), but the people had gotten so accustomed to their blessings that they detested it and called it "this good-for-nothing bread." (See Num. 11:4–6.)

What does John 6 tell us about the manna? In what ways was manna a type (foreshadow, picture) of Jesus Christ? How was the people's rejection of the manna a rejection of the Son of God?

From the Commentary

Leaving the field of battle, Israel continued to march north, crossing the Zared River and camping there. Then they crossed the Arnon River and approached the country of the Amorites, traveling between Moabite and Amorite country. In Numbers 22—24, we'll meet the Moabites again and see how they tricked Israel into disobeying God.

In 21:14–15, we have a description of the area, taken from an ancient record called *The Book of the Wars of the Lord.* This lost book was apparently a compendium of detailed information about the travels and the battles of Israel. Here it is quoted to describe the geography of the area through which Israel was then passing. It was not comfortable terrain, but the Lord gave His people the strength they needed to make the journey.

When they arrived at Beer ("well"), the Lord anticipated the nation's need and promised to give them water. (See Ex. 17:1–7; Num. 20:2–13; 21:5.) "What shall we eat?" and "What shall we drink?" seemed to be the major concerns of the people (Matt. 6:24–34), just as they are the major concerns of people today, along with "What shall we wear?" But on this occasion, the people didn't complain. Instead, they sang a song! As far as the record is concerned, this is the first time we find Israel singing since God delivered them from Egypt forty years before (Ex. 15).

"The Song of the Well" (Num. 21:16–18) celebrated the Lord's provision of water for the people in the wilderness. It's not likely that the leaders of Israel actually dug the well with their staffs (NIV), because in the sandy wasteland they would have needed much better tools. Since this is a song, we must leave room for poetic expression. What may have happened is that God showed Moses where the water was located, the leaders all thrust their staffs into the ground around that place, and the well opened up and the water gushed out.

—*Be Counted*, pages 118–119

10. Review Numbers 21:10–20. Why did the people rejoice? We've seen a picture of Jesus in the manna as the Bread of Life (John 6); how is He also found in the well? (See John 7:37–39.) What is the symbolic meaning of the uplifted serpent in Numbers 21:4–9 and John 3:14?

Looking Inward

Take a moment to reflect on all that you've explored thus far in this study of Numbers 18—21. Review your notes and answers and think about how each of these things matters in your life today.

Tips for Small Groups: To get the most out of this section, form pairs or trios and have group members take turns answering these questions. Be honest and as open as you can in this discussion, but most of all, be encouraging and supportive of others. Be sensitive to those who are going through particularly difficult times and don't press for people to speak if they're uncomfortable doing so.

11. How do you support the leaders in your life? How does supporting the leaders who influence you help you to grow in faith?

12. Have you ever wanted to quit while doing something you know God has asked you to do? Why or why not? What prompts that defeated feeling? What lessons can you learn from the way Moses responded to his own failure?

13. What are some ways you see Jesus in the everyday? How can thankfulness for the necessities of life turn you toward praise? What are some ways you praise God for the little things?

Going Forward

14. Think of one or two things that you have learned that you'd like to work on in the coming week. Remember that this is all about quality, not quantity. It's better to work on one specific area of life and do it well than to work on many and do poorly (or to be so overwhelmed that you simply don't try).

Do you want to learn what God has been teaching you with past defeats? Be specific. Go back through Numbers 18—21 and put a star next to the phrase or verse that is most encouraging to you. Consider memorizing this verse.

Real-Life Application Ideas: This week, turn your attention to the simple things in life that point us toward Jesus—things like food, water, shelter. Then look for a practical way to help others in one of those areas. Work at a soup kitchen, deliver food to a friend or neighbor, offer your home to someone who needs a place to stay. By doing these things, you'll be exemplifying Christ and giving others the opportunity to taste Jesus' love in a practical way.

Seeking Help

15. Write a prayer below (or simply pray one in silence), inviting God to work on your mind and heart in those areas you've noted in the Going Forward section. Be honest about your desires and fears.

Notes for Small Groups:

- *Look for ways to put into practice the things you wrote in the Going Forward section. Talk with other group members about your ideas and commit to being accountable to one another.*
- *During the coming week, ask the Holy Spirit to continue to reveal truth to you from what you've read and studied.*
- *Before you start the next lesson, read Numbers 22—25. For more in-depth lesson preparation, read chapters 9 and 10, "Principalities and Powers—Part I," and "Principalities and Powers—Part II," in* Be Counted.

Principalities
(NUMBERS 22—25)

Before you begin …

- *Pray for the Holy Spirit to reveal truth and wisdom as you go through this lesson.*
- *Read Numbers 22—25. This lesson references chapters 9 and 10 in* Be Counted. *It will be helpful for you to have your Bible and a copy of the commentary available as you work through this lesson.*

Getting Started

From the Commentary

On Passover night, the people of Israel marched out of Egypt like conquering soldiers, and God buried the pursuing Egyptian army under the waters of the Red Sea. Except for the Canaanites that Israel rashly attacked out of the will of God (Num. 14:39–45), every enemy Israel encountered, they defeated: Amalek (Ex. 17:8–16), the king of Arad (Num. 21:1–3), the Amorites (vv. 21–25), and the forces of Og, king of Bashan (vv. 33–35).

> But when Israel arrived on the plains of Moab, they faced a different kind of enemy, one who was hidden in the mountain heights and able to call upon the forces of the Evil One to assist him. Camping peacefully in the valley, the Israelites had no idea that Balaam was trying to curse them so that the Moabites and Midianites could defeat them. This scenario reminds us of Paul's warning in Ephesians 6:12, "For we wrestle not against flesh and blood, but against principalities, against powers, against the rulers of the darkness of this world [age], against spiritual wickedness in high [heavenly] places."
>
> —*Be Counted,* page 127

1. How was the circumstance the Israelites faced with Balaam similar to what Paul wrote about in 2 Corinthians 11:3 and Peter wrote about in 1 Peter 5:8? What are the "principalities and powers" that God protected Israel from while they camped on the plains of Moab?

More to Consider: The key performer in this drama is a mysterious soothsayer named Balaam, a Gentile who lived at a place called Pethor near the Euphrates River (Num. 22:5; Deut. 23:4). He had a reputation for success in divination (receiving hidden knowledge, especially about the future) and incantation (the use of occult power to grant blessing or cursing), and he was willing to sell his services to any who could pay his fee. Why are all of these details important to the story? Who are today's "soothsayers"? In what ways are they a threat to our churches?

2. Choose one verse or phrase from Numbers 22—25 that stands out to you. This could be something you're intrigued by, something that makes you uncomfortable, something that puzzles you, something that resonates with you, or just something you want to examine further. Write that here.

Going Deeper

From the Commentary

The Moabites and Midianites became very frightened when they saw the magnitude of the camp of Israel ("they cover the face of the earth," Num. 22:5) and heard the reports of Israel's military victories over the neighboring nations ("as an ox licks up the grass of the field," v. 4 NKJV). Balak, king of Moab, didn't realize that God had told Israel not to attack Moab (Deut. 2:9) because the Moabites were relatives of the Jews, being descendants of Abraham's nephew Lot (Gen. 19:26–37).

Conventional warfare was out of the question. Moab and Midian needed the help of the Devil, and Balaam was in touch with the Devil. This confrontation would be another episode in what Donald Grey Barnhouse called "the invisible war," the conflict between the Lord and Satan that began when God cursed the serpent in the garden (3:13–15; see Rev. 12). Balaam must have had a wide reputation as a successful practitioner of occult arts, otherwise Balak wouldn't have ignored both distance and price when he sent for him.

Balak depended on two things to influence Balaam to come and help him: the impressive delegation of important elders from both Midian and Moab, and the wealth they carried to pay his fee. Balaam was definitely a hireling who was interested primarily in money (2 Peter 2:15). Though twice he refused to accept Balak's summons, Balaam deceptively maneuvered around God's declared will so that he could go to Moab and receive his fee.

In those days, people believed that each nation had its own god, and Balaam knew that Jehovah was the God of the Israelites. Therefore, he went to seek the Lord's will about the summons from Balak. It was God who came to Balaam, not Balaam who brought God to himself, and

> the Lord wouldn't allow him to accept the invitation. God made His will very clear: "Do not go with them. You must not put a curse on those people, because they are blessed" (Num. 22:12 NIV). Balaam knew that without the God of Israel on his side, he would fail in his assignment, so he told the delegation he wouldn't go with them. *However, he didn't tell them the reason: Israel couldn't be cursed because God had blessed them.*
>
> —*Be Counted*, pages 128–129

3. What, ultimately, convinced Balaam to agree to Balak's offer (Num. 22:16–20)? Balaam clearly believed God existed, so why did Balaam think he could circumvent God's will? How do we do the same thing sometimes in today's church?

From the Commentary

> God was angry at Balaam for defying His will and allowing the love of money to control him. We sometimes use the phrase *dumb animals,* but in this case the animal was smarter than her master and his two servants! She saw

the angel of the Lord holding a sword and blocking the way, and by turning aside, she saved Balaam's life. Three times she changed the route and three times her master beat her. Balaam was beside himself with anger, and had he been armed, he would have killed his faithful beast. Peter called it "the madness of the prophet" (2 Peter 2:16).

Why wasn't Balaam shocked when his beast spoke to him "with a man's voice" (v. 16 NIV)? This certainly wasn't an everyday occurrence even for a professional soothsayer. Satan spoke through a serpent when he deceived Eve (Gen. 3:1ff.; 2 Cor. 11:3), and it's possible that in the past Satan's demons had spoken to Balaam through animals. A person has reached a very low level in life if God has to use brute beasts to communicate His mind.

The same God who opened the donkey's mouth and eyes also opened Balaam's eyes so he could see the awesome angel standing in the road, his sword in hand. Balaam finally did something right and fell on his face before the angel, who told him that his beast had saved his life. The angel warned Balaam that he was rushing headlong and recklessly on a wrong path that could only lead to ruin, and Balaam offered to return home.

—*Be Counted*, pages 130–131

4. Were Balaam's words, "I have sinned," evidence of sincere repentance? Why or why not? Read Exodus 9:27 (Pharaoh); 1 Samuel 15:24, 30; 26:21 (King Saul); and Matthew 27:4 (Judas). How were each of these characters'

words similar to Balaam's? What does true confession sound like? (See 2 Sam. 12:13–23; 24:10, 17; 1 Chron. 21:8, 17; Ps. 54:4.)

From the Commentary

> For the king to hasten out to meet the commoner shows how anxious Balak was to get started in his attack against Israel. Why had Balaam delayed his coming? Wasn't Balak's offer generous enough? Didn't the prophet realize the seriousness of the situation? Balaam didn't defend himself or explain his actions, but he did state clearly that all he could do was declare the words God gave him. The king offered sacrifices to his god Baal and probably gave Balaam some of the inner parts of the animals to use for divination.
>
> The next morning, Balak took Balaam to Bamoth Baal ("the high places of Baal") where they could see the camp of Israel and offer more sacrifices to Baal. Balaam used these sacrifices as part of his sorcery and soothsaying (Num. 24:1) and didn't simply wait for God's promised message.
>
> —*Be Counted*, page 131

5. Why did God endure Balaam's duplicity? How does this reveal God's grace and goodness? What was the message God wanted to deliver through Balaam? How did that message ultimately get delivered? What was Balak's response?

From the Commentary

> To encourage Balaam to do what he was hired to do—curse Israel—Balak asked his hired prophet to get a different perspective. He took him to the top of Mount Pisgah where again they offered sacrifices to their gods (Num. 23:13–14; see Deut. 34:1–4). The fact that Balaam participated in these pagan occult rituals shows the wickedness of his heart. He spoke the Word of God and longed for a righteous death, yet he thought nothing of using enchantments and consorting with Satan (Num. 24:1). He was a double-minded man whose chief desire was to make as much money as possible by marketing his skills.
>
> The first oracle pictured Israel as a *chosen people* because of the love of God, and the second oracle presents them as a *conquering people* because of the faithfulness of God. God

> doesn't lie, so all His promises and covenants are sure; He doesn't change, so His character remains the same. He isn't weak but is able to fulfill what He promises; nobody can manipulate Him or control Him. God was with the people of Israel and reigned as their King.
>
> It was God who gave Israel their victories, beginning with their exodus from Egypt. The nation was like an ox in its strength and like a lioness and a lion in its determination to catch its prey and kill it. Therefore, no sorcery could succeed against God's people because God was at work in them and through them. "Oh, what God has done!" (Num. 23:23 NKJV).
>
> —*Be Counted*, pages 133–134

6. What did God see when He looked upon Israel? (See Ex. 19:6.) Who are God's chosen people today? (See Eph. 1:4; 1 Pet. 2:5, 9–10.) How does God deal with His chosen people when they disobey? When they follow Him?

From the Commentary

> The emphasis in Numbers 23:27—24:14 is on the contentment of God's people in their own land. The conquest of Canaan is over (Num. 24:8–9), their enemies have been defeated, and Israel is enjoying the abundance of God's provision in "the land of milk and honey." The Promised Land is a paradise with an abundance of water, an important commodity in the East, and Israel's dwelling places are situated like beautiful flowers and trees in a garden. Beauty and bounty are seen in the land because of the blessing of the Lord.
>
> In the second oracle, Balaam saw God as Israel's King (23:21), but now he sees the nation ruled by its own king who is greater than Agag (24:7). Since the name Agag shows up centuries later (1 Sam. 15:9), it may have been the official name of the rulers of the Amalekites, such as "Pharaoh" in Egypt and "Abimelech" in Gerar (Gen. 20; 26). When Israel was on the way to Sinai, the Amalekites attacked them and were defeated by Moses' prayers and Joshua's soldiers, and the Amalekites became the sworn enemies of the Jews (Ex. 17:8–16).
>
> —*Be Counted*, pages 139–140

7. Which Jewish king might be referred to in the prophecy of 24:7? How is this king a type of Jesus Christ? (See Ps. 89:27.) What is the promise of this prophecy regarding the land of Israel? (See Isa. 35.)

From the Commentary

The preface in 24:15–19 is similar to that of the third oracle (Num. 24:3–4), emphasizing that what Balaam saw and heard came from the Lord. It was so overwhelming that it left the prophet prostrate on the ground. You would think that such a remarkable experience with the living God would have brought Balaam to the place of submission and faith, but it did not. It only shows how close an unbeliever can come to the knowledge of the Lord and still reject the truth (Matt. 7:15–23).

The vision is brief and to the point; it focuses on the coming Messiah of Israel and His conquests "in the latter days" (Num. 24:14). The images of the star and scepter speak of Messiah's kingship and reign (Gen. 49:10; Rev. 22:16), and "out of Jacob shall come he who shall have dominion" certainly refers to Messiah (Num. 24:19; Ps. 72:8; Zech. 9:10; Rev. 1:6). While a part of this vision may have been fulfilled in a lesser way in the conquests of David, Jesus the Son of David will fulfill them completely when He returns to conquer His enemies and establish His kingdom on the earth (Rev. 19:11—20:6).

But the soothsayer wasn't finished. As he stood on the top of Peor, he had visions concerning other nations and predicted their destiny. *Amalek* (Num. 24:20) was the first nation to attack Israel after their exodus from Egypt (Ex. 17:8–16), but they would be finally defeated and wiped out by David (1 Sam. 27:8–9; 2 Sam. 8:11–12). *The Kenites* (Num. 24:21–22) were a nomadic people who

> lived among the Midianites. They lived in the mountainous regions, but their "nest" wouldn't protect them from the invading Assyrians (Asshur), who would take them captive. The fate of the nations is in God's hands (Acts 17:24–28), and no nation or individual could survive apart from His mercy (Num. 24:23).
>
> The predictions in verse 24 are difficult to interpret, but as Dr. Roland B. Allen states, "[O]ne nation will rise and supplant another, only to face its own doom. In contrast there is the implied ongoing blessing on the people of Israel and their sure promise of a future deliverer who will have the final victory."
>
> —*Be Counted*, pages 140–141

8. Why did God give these visions to a covetous Gentile soothsayer instead of to a dedicated Jewish prophet? (See Isa. 55:8–11.) What is surprising about the way Balaam responded to these visions?

From the Commentary

> Balaam wasn't able to curse Israel, but he knew how to defile them and seduce them into sin so great that Jehovah would judge them. Balaam suggested to Balak (Num. 31:16) that the Moabites (25:1) and Midianites (v. 6) convene a religious feast to honor Baal, and that they invite the Jews to attend. The feast, of course, would involve idolatry and abominable immorality and would be a flagrant violation of Israel's covenant with the Lord. But Moab was related to Israel through Abraham's nephew Lot, and the Midianites were the allies of Moab, so there was no reason why the Jews shouldn't be "neighborly." What Balaam couldn't do by appealing to the demons, he accomplished by appealing to the flesh and inviting the Jews to "enjoy themselves" at Baal Peor.
>
> —*Be Counted*, page 142

9. This is the first recorded occasion in Scripture of Israel worshipping Baal, but it certainly isn't the last. Why were they so easily tempted to worship Baal in this situation? Why didn't they turn down the invitation to participate? What did God's law have to say about the idolatry and the immorality practiced by the Moabites and Midianites? (See Ex. 20:1–5, 14.)

More to Consider: God declared that the Midianites were to be considered the enemies of Israel and had to be killed. The account of Moses' fulfilling this order is in Numbers 31:1–24. As we've already noted, Balaam, the man who masterminded the feast, was killed at the same time.

It's easy to criticize the Lord and Scripture because of these national massacres, but God had His reasons. (See Gen. 15:16.) He had given them time to repent. He had revealed Himself to them in nature (Rom. 1:18–32; Ps. 19), and they had heard of the Lord's judgments against Egypt (Josh. 2:8–14). What does God's decision to destroy the nation reveal about His patience? His plan? His belief in Israel? How was God removing a temptation for the Israelites by destroying the Midianites?

From the Commentary

> As God's people today, we must not think that the Old Testament narratives are past history and simply interesting stories for us to read. Until the New Testament was written, the only Scripture the first-century church had was the Old Testament, and from it they were able to get encouragement and enlightenment. These events in Jewish history serve as warnings to us not to disobey the Lord (1 Cor. 10:1–13) as well as encouragements to build our faith (Heb. 11) and hope (Rom. 15:4).
>
> Balaam is mentioned by three different New Testament writers: Peter (2 Peter 2:15–16), Jude (v. 11), and John (Rev. 2:14).
>
> —*Be Counted*, page 144

10. Review 2 Peter 2:15–16, verse 11 of Jude, and Revelation 2:14. What are the warnings offered by Peter and Jude? What aspect of Balaam's doctrine is warned against in Revelation?

Looking Inward

Take a moment to reflect on all that you've explored thus far in this study of Numbers 22—25. Review your notes and answers and think about how each of these things matters in your life today.

Tips for Small Groups: To get the most out of this section, form pairs or trios and have group members take turns answering these questions. Be honest and as open as you can in this discussion, but most of all, be encouraging and supportive of others. Be sensitive to those who are going through particularly difficult times and don't press for people to speak if they're uncomfortable doing so.

11. Have you ever encountered God in a surprising way (as Balaam did with the donkey)? Describe that situation. What was God trying to tell you? What was your response?

12. Balaam was given ample opportunity to truly follow God and turn away from his false gods, but he chose not to. Has there ever been a time when God appealed to you and you turned Him away? Discuss that experience. What temptations kept you from trusting God?

13. Balaam's story is one of a few in the Bible where God used a nonbeliever to deliver His truth. How has God used nonbelievers to help you grow closer to Him? Why does God use people who don't believe in Him to deliver His truth?

Going Forward

14. Think of one or two things that you have learned that you'd like to work on in the coming week. Remember that this is all about quality, not quantity. It's better to work on one specific area of life and do it well than

to work on many and do poorly (or to be so overwhelmed that you simply don't try).

Do you want to discern if you are being tempted by any false gods? Be specific. Go back through Numbers 22—25 and put a star next to the phrase or verse that is most encouraging to you. Consider memorizing this verse.

Real-Life Application Ideas: The Israelites were quick to fall into bad habits, choosing to worship Baal instead of the one true God. This week, take inventory of the things that tempt you away from God. Talk with your small group leader or a church leader about those things and how to gird yourself against falling for those temptations. Then soak this week in prayer, asking God to give you the wisdom and strength to follow Him and avoid falling for bad habits.

Seeking Help

15. Write a prayer below (or simply pray one in silence), inviting God to work on your mind and heart in those areas you've noted in the Going Forward section. Be honest about your desires and fears.

Notes for Small Groups:

- *Look for ways to put into practice the things you wrote in the Going Forward section. Talk with other group members about your ideas and commit to being accountable to one another.*
- *During the coming week, ask the Holy Spirit to continue to reveal truth to you from what you've read and studied.*
- *Before you start the next lesson, read Numbers 26—29, 36. For more in-depth lesson preparation, read chapter 11, "A New Beginning," in* Be Counted.

A New Beginning

(NUMBERS 26—29, 36)

Before you begin …

- *Pray for the Holy Spirit to reveal truth and wisdom as you go through this lesson.*
- *Read Numbers 26—29, 36. This lesson references chapter 11 in* Be Counted. *It will be helpful for you to have your Bible and a copy of the commentary available as you work through this lesson.*

Getting Started

From the Commentary

The transition between chapters 25 and 26 reminds us of the transition from chapter 14 to chapter 15, for in both of them the Lord moved from judgment to mercy, from punishment to promise. At Kadesh-Barnea and at Baal Peor, Israel had sinned greatly and God chastened them, but in His grace He forgave their disobedience and gave them a new start.

—*Be Counted,* page 151

1. Read Ezra 9:13. How does this passage express the feelings of the Israelites after God's shift from judgment to mercy? How do David's words in Psalm 103:10 also reflect this sentiment? How easy is it for us to have this attitude? Why does God continue to give His people second chances? What does this tell us about God's character?

2. Choose one verse or phrase from Numbers 26—29, 36 that stands out to you. This could be something you're intrigued by, something that makes you uncomfortable, something that puzzles you, something that resonates with you, or just something you want to examine further. Write that here.

Going Deeper

From the Commentary

> By the time Israel had entered the Zared valley (Num. 21:12), the old generation had died off (Deut. 2:14–15), except for Moses, Caleb, and Joshua (Num. 26:63–65), and very soon, Moses would die. Israel was making a new beginning, thanks to the faithfulness and mercy of God. It was time to take a census of the new generation and start looking toward the future.
>
> —*Be Counted*, pages 151–152

3. Review Numbers 26:1–56. What purposes did Moses have in mind when he took the second census? What were the military reasons? The inheritance-related reasons?

More to Consider: The first census had revealed a total of 603,550 available soldiers (1:45–46), while the second census totaled 601,730 (26:51), a slight decrease. What does this little detail reveal about God's care for His people during their exodus? How does this show that God kept His covenant promise? (See Gen. 12:2; 15:5; 22:17.)

From the Commentary

> God could have sent angels to clean up Canaan instantly, but He chose to work through human beings, a day at a time. God is certainly longsuffering toward His people, and we ought to count it a great privilege to know Him and be able to work with Him in doing His work.
>
> —*Be Counted*, page 153

4. God has sometimes used dramatic and supernatural events to accomplish His will. Why did He choose a more down-to-earth approach in this season of the Israelites' history? How might that have helped to develop the people's faith?

From Today's World

The Israelites were given more than a few "fresh starts," though none quite so dramatic as their entrance into the Promised Land. God had proven to be faithful to His promise but had also shown His ability to forgive and forget. In today's highly connected world, fresh starts are a little more complex, since many of our choices and words are recorded for perpetuity. Men and women who have public faces have an especially hard time starting over once they've fallen from grace, but this is also true of the common man and woman, thanks to Facebook and Twitter and the ubiquity of the Internet.

5. In the modern age, past sins are often held over our heads by those we have hurt or by those who want to hurt us. How do we move forward into a "new beginning" when others are so inclined to remind us of our sins? How does God's forgiveness look different to His followers today than it did to those in Moses' time?

From the Commentary

> Israel had not yet crossed the river and entered the Promised Land, and yet by faith Moses was already preparing for the tribes to claim their land. (The words

> *inherit* or *inheritance* are used twelve times in this section.) Except for fulfilling God's command to wipe out the Midianites (Num. 25:16–18; 31:1–11), Israel would have no more battles until they arrived at Jericho. Though he wasn't allowed to go in himself, Moses invested the closing weeks of his life in preparing the new generation to enter Canaan and claim the land God promised to give them.
>
> —*Be Counted*, page 153

6. Underline the uses of the word *inherit* or *inheritance* in Numbers 26:52—27:11; 36. What are the obvious implications of this repeated theme? What are the different kinds of inheritance described here? Why was this such an important theme for the wandering Israelites?

From the Commentary

> To the Jews in Canaan, possessing land was the foundation for building a family, earning an income, and having security and the necessities of life. The prophets frequently denounced wealthy people who amassed great

> estates by stealing land from the poor (Isa. 5:8–10; Mic. 2:1–3; Hab. 2:9–12). The ideal life for an Old Testament Jew was to own his own land and be able to sit under his own fig tree and enjoy his family and the fruit of his labor (1 Kings 4:25; Mic. 4:4).
>
> —*Be Counted*, page 156

7. How does today's ideal life compare to that of the Old Testament Jew? What can we learn from their ideal life that we can apply to our own goals and dreams? How did God honor the Jews' dreams of a good life? How does He honor our dreams of a good life too?

From the Commentary

> Though still physically strong, Moses was now 120 years old (Deut. 31:2; 34:7), and the time had come for him to move off the scene. He had led the people of Israel faithfully for forty years (Acts 7:23, 30; Ex. 7:7), bearing their burdens, sharing their victories, and teaching them God's laws. God and Moses communed with each other

> as friend with friend, and the Lord didn't hide anything from His servant.
>
> Because Moses and Aaron had not honored the Lord at Meribah, they weren't permitted to enter the Promised Land with the new generation (Num. 20:2–13). Moses repeatedly asked God for permission to enter the land (Deut. 3:23–29), but the Lord refused to relent. Not only must Moses be disciplined because of his pride and anger at Meribah, but he must not mar the type that would be expounded in the book of Hebrews. It isn't the law (Moses) that gives us our spiritual inheritance but Jesus (Joshua; Heb. 4:8; and context).
>
> After Moses delivered the messages recorded in Deuteronomy, he was permitted to ascend Mount Nebo (Pisgah) in the Abarim mountain range, and view the land that Israel would inherit (Deut. 32:48–52; 34:1–4). Centuries later, Moses and Elijah would stand in glory on the Mount of Transfiguration when they talked with Jesus about His impending death on the cross (Matt. 17:1–8), so he did finally make it to the Promised Land.
>
> —*Be Counted*, pages 156–157

8. Review Numbers 27:12–14. Why didn't God choose to forgive Moses and Aaron for their misdeeds? What message was God giving His people by sticking to the decision not to allow Moses and Aaron into the Promised Land?

More to Consider: Why was Joshua the man God chose to take Moses' place? Read these passages to find out: Exodus 17:8–16; 24:13; 32:17; 33:11; Numbers 11:28; 14:6–9; 27:18; Deuteronomy 34:9. What does this teach us about the kind of character that God wants in His leaders?

From the Commentary

During his years of service with Moses, Joshua learned some valuable principles of spiritual life and service, principles that still apply today. When you read the book of Joshua, you see that he was concerned for the glory of God and the welfare of the people, and that he was careful to obey the orders God gave him. The two times Joshua didn't seek God's will, he brought the nation into shameful defeat (Josh. 7 and 9), but to his credit, he trusted God to make his mistakes work out successfully in the end.

Under Joshua's leadership, the nation worked together to defeat the pagan nations in Canaan and then establish the nation of Israel. Before he died, he called the leaders and the people together and led them in dedicating themselves and their families to the Lord, affirming to them, "As for me and my house, we will serve the LORD" (24:15).

—*Be Counted*, page 158

9. One of the responsibilities of Christian leaders today is to see to it that the next generation is equipped to carry on the work (2 Tim. 2:2). How was Joshua prepared to take over as leader? What lessons had he learned in the course of the forty years of wandering?

From the Commentary

> From the beginning of their national life, the secret of Israel's success was a relationship to the Lord characterized by faith and obedience. The Jews were God's covenant people, chosen by Him to do His will and ultimately bring the Redeemer into the world. Once Israel was settled in the land, they had to be careful to follow these instructions carefully, for they worshipped the Lord God Almighty. The pagan nations around them could invent their own forms of worship, but Israel had to bring the right sacrifices at the right time and in the right way, or the Lord could not bless them (John 4:22).
>
> Some of the instructions given here had already been given at Sinai, while others were new. The basis for their worship was the calendar of special days outlined in Leviticus 23, beginning with the weekly Sabbath and ending with

> the annual Feast of Tabernacles. Each of the offerings had a different purpose to fulfill, but the ultimate goal was to please the Lord and delight His heart. God seeks for true worshippers (John 4:23) and delights in the worship of His loving people.
>
> —*Be Counted*, pages 158–159

10. What are some of the different ways the Israelites worshipped God in their new land? What were some of the regular practices that honored God?

Looking Inward

Take a moment to reflect on all that you've explored thus far in this study of Numbers 26—29, 36. Review your notes and answers and think about how each of these things matters in your life today.

Tips for Small Groups: To get the most out of this section, form pairs or trios and have group members take turns answering these questions. Be honest and as open as you can in this discussion, but most of all, be encouraging and supportive of others. Be sensitive to those who are going through particularly difficult times and don't press for people to speak if they're uncomfortable doing so.

11. Do you sometimes feel judged by God? Why? Describe a time when you felt God's mercy. What did that teach you about God's judgment? In what ways does God's mercy bring you closer to Him?

12. How does it feel when you are granted a new beginning? What new beginnings has God given you? What is your responsibility when you've been given a fresh start?

13. The Israelites began to worship God in a new way once they were in the Promised Land. What are some ways you have learned to worship God that show you've grown in your faith?

Going Forward

14. Think of one or two things that you have learned that you'd like to work on in the coming week. Remember that this is all about quality, not quantity. It's better to work on one specific area of life and do it well than to work on many and do poorly (or to be so overwhelmed that you simply don't try).

Do you want to become more aware of God's mercy toward you? Be specific. Go back through Numbers 26—29, 36 and put a star next to the phrase or verse that is most encouraging to you. Consider memorizing this verse.

Real-Life Application Ideas: Make this a week of worship. You may want to spend some time focusing on different areas in your life that you're thankful for (family, friends, work, etc.). But be sure to also include a time for thanking God just for being God.

Seeking Help

15. Write a prayer below (or simply pray one in silence), inviting God to work on your mind and heart in those areas you've noted in the Going Forward section. Be honest about your desires and fears.

Notes for Small Groups:

- *Look for ways to put into practice the things you wrote in the Going Forward section. Talk with other group members about your ideas and commit to being accountable to one another.*
- *During the coming week, ask the Holy Spirit to continue to reveal truth to you from what you've read and studied.*
- *Before you start the next lesson, read Numbers 30—35. For more in-depth lesson preparation, read chapter 12, "Preparing for Conquest," in* Be Counted.

Preparation

(NUMBERS 30—35)

Before you begin …

- *Pray for the Holy Spirit to reveal truth and wisdom as you go through this lesson.*
- *Read Numbers 30—35. This lesson references chapter 12 in* Be Counted. *It will be helpful for you to have your Bible and a copy of the commentary available as you work through this lesson.*

Getting Started

From the Commentary

For forty years, Israel had been moving from place to place, a nomadic people traveling to their Promised Land. Soon they would enter and conquer that land and establish their own nation, and for this responsibility they had to be prepared. The final chapters of Numbers, along with the book of Deuteronomy, record the Lord's instructions through Moses, given to prepare the people for this challenging new experience. For Israel to become

> a holy nation to the glory of God, they had to accept and apply the basic principles Moses enunciated, and these principles still work in communities and nations today.
>
> —*Be Counted,* page 165

1. What kind of preparation did Moses introduce in these chapters? What are some of the principles Moses taught the Israelites that are still applicable today?

2. Choose one verse or phrase from Numbers 30—35 that stands out to you. This could be something you're intrigued by, something that makes you uncomfortable, something that puzzles you, something that resonates with you, or just something you want to examine further. Write that here.

Going Deeper

From the Commentary

> In Leviticus 27 Moses had touched on the subject of vows in terms of dedicating people and possessions to the Lord,

> but here he deals with personal vows and how they are affected by relationships. The chapter makes it clear that the home is basic to the nation, that there must be authority and subordination in the home, and that truth is what binds society together.
>
> —*Be Counted*, page 165

3. Review Numbers 30:1–16. What is the difference between a vow and an oath? What role does God play in both? What happens when people forget that God hears everything they say and knows everything they do? (See Deut. 23:21; Ps. 76:11; Eccl. 5:1–7.)

More to Consider: When the men made promises to God, they had to keep their promises and nobody could annul them, but what about the women? Read Numbers 30:3–15. What do these verses reveal about the vows of single women, women formerly married, and married women? What role did a woman's father or husband play in the vows? Is this different today? Explain.

From the Commentary

If the father hears a vow from a single woman at home and says nothing, the vow must stand and the young woman must fulfill it. Not only is there power in words, but there's also power in silence; in this case, silence means consent. But if the father announces that he disapproves of the vow, then the vow is canceled. If later she becomes engaged to be married and her fiancé knows about the vow and says nothing, then the vow stands, even after they marry, but if he doesn't approve, the vow is annulled even if her father approved it. The Lord would then release her from the obligations related to that vow.

When it comes to the widow and the divorcee, the Lord assumes that these women are experienced and mature and can make wise decisions, although age and experience aren't always a guarantee of wisdom. If they make promises to the Lord, these promises must be fulfilled. Moses doesn't explain what would happen if they married again. Since no special qualifications are given, we assume that their vows couldn't be canceled even by their new husbands.

If the husband hears his wife's vow and says nothing, the vow becomes binding, for silence means consent. If he openly disagrees with the vow and forbids it, the vow is annulled. However, if he should change his mind after consenting, then he (not the wife) must pay the penalty for causing her to abandon her sacred vow, and this meant bringing a sin offering to the Lord (Lev. 5:4).

—*Be Counted*, pages 166–167

4. Why are there so many rules about women and vows? What are the universal messages in these instructions that go beyond gender issues? What does it mean to make a promise to another person?

From Today's World

The Old Testament is full of rules that apply differently to men and women. And while the New Testament introduces equality in terms of how God sees men and women, it also differentiates between the sexes in other ways. While some of these are certainly cultural issues and not relevant today, others have been the source of debate in the church for years. Even today, churches vary dramatically in the way they view women, particularly in leadership roles.

5. Why do churches vary so much in the way they honor or treat women? What are the most controversial issues related to women in the church? How does Jesus' teaching speak to the universal truths about men and women in the church? Should there be differences in how men and women are treated? Why or why not?

From the Commentary

> Though the people of Israel were wrong in getting entangled with the Midianites at Baal Peor, Midian was wrong in following Balaam's counsel and trying to destroy Israel. Those who curse Israel, God will curse (Gen. 12:1–3), and the time had come for God to punish Midian (Num. 25:16–18).
>
> —*Be Counted*, page 167

6. Review Numbers 31. How was the battle at Midian a sort of dress rehearsal for the fight in the land of Canaan? This would be Moses' last battle. What legacy did he leave the Israelites? How was he honored?

From the Commentary

> The battle described in 31:1–10 was part of a "holy war" that Jehovah had declared against Midian because Midian had led Israel into sin. Certainly Israel was responsible for disobeying God and engaging in idolatry and immorality, and God punished them for it, but Midian was the

> chief offender, and such offenses must be punished (Matt. 18:7). The church has no mandate from God to engage in "holy wars" (John 18:10–11, 36) because our enemies aren't flesh and blood (Eph. 6:10ff.) and our weapons are spiritual (2 Cor. 10:1–6). The sword of the Spirit is the only sword we use to advance the cause of Christ (Eph. 6:17–18).
>
> —*Be Counted*, page 168

7. What was the result of the battle with the Midianites? (See Num. 31:7, 48–49.) In this battle, Israel received their instructions from God and trusted God to go before them and give them victory. How does this same pattern continue elsewhere in Scripture?

From the Commentary

> In disobedience to God's command, the soldiers did not exterminate all the Midianites, but brought the women and children back as captives. This angered Moses, for the presence of the Midianite women and girls in the camp only gave further opportunity for the sin that had almost

> destroyed Israel. The nation had won the battle but was now in danger of losing the victory, a mistake that God's people have made more than once down through the centuries.
>
> Moses commanded that the male children be slain as well as the women and girls who were not virgins. The virgins remaining could be taken by the men to be servants. Since the soldiers had been defiled in battle by touching dead bodies, they had to obey the law of cleansing (Num. 19:11–13), and Moses applied this same rule to the female captives who were now expected to obey Jewish law. The great amount of wealth that was taken from Midian also had to be purified, either by fire or by the water of cleansing, and it would take a week for this purification to be completed.
>
> —*Be Counted*, pages 168–169

8. This is a difficult passage to read. Why would God be upset that the women and children were taken captive rather than killed? Why was obedience so important to the relationship between God and His people? Why didn't God allow compromise in this situation? What was the result of their disobedience?

More to Consider: The people and animals Israel took as spoils of war were distributed three ways: The soldiers got half, the people in the camp got half, and both the soldiers and the people gave a percentage to the Lord. How is this similar to the lessons taught in the New Testament about stewardship? How is it different?

From the Commentary

> The Lord commanded Moses to keep a list of the places Israel camped during their wilderness journey. Forty places are listed, starting with Rameses in Egypt (Num. 33:3) and ending with the plains of Moab, across from Jericho (v. 49). Israel's exodus from Egypt is recorded in verses 3–4, and their march to and through the Red Sea in verses 5–8. Verses 9–15 take Israel from Marah to Mount Sinai, and verses 16–36 from Sinai to Kadesh, where, because of their unbelief, Israel failed to enter the Promised Land. Their thirty-eight years of wandering fall between verses 36 and 37 and are graciously passed over in silence. The passage from Kadesh to the plains of Moab is recorded in verses 37–49.
>
> —*Be Counted*, page 173

9. Review Numbers 33:1–49. In what ways is this chapter more than just a list of places? What testimony does it provide about the sovereignty of God? What are other examples in biblical history where God provided for His people? How does He provide in a similar way for His people today?

From the Commentary

> The land of Canaan is mentioned sixteen times in 33:50—35:34, and the emphasis is on Israel entering the land and claiming the promised inheritance. The Lord wanted the people to know that the thirty-eight-year delay didn't alter His plans or annul His promises. The section opens with the Lord saying, "When you have crossed the Jordan into the land of Canaan" (Num. 33:51 NKJV). What an encouragement that statement was to them!
>
> God wanted Israel's invasion of Canaan to be a total conquest. Israel was to drive out and dispossess the inhabitants, destroy the altars, images, and temples, and then divide the land among the tribes. The command was nothing new, because the Lord had told them this at Sinai (Ex. 23:20–33; 34:10–17).
>
> —*Be Counted*, pages 174–175

10. Review Numbers 33:50—35:34. What were the reasons for total conquest of Canaan? (See Gen. 15:14–16; Lev. 18:24–28; Num. 33:54–56.) How does Moses' farewell message underscore the command to drive out the inhabitants? (See Deut. 7; 12:1–3.) In what ways does this seemingly brutal command reveal God's love for His people?

Looking Inward

Take a moment to reflect on all that you've explored thus far in this study of Numbers 30—35. Review your notes and answers and think about how each of these things matters in your life today.

Tips for Small Groups: To get the most out of this section, form pairs or trios and have group members take turns answering these questions. Be honest and as open as you can in this discussion, but most of all, be encouraging and supportive of others. Be sensitive to those who are going through particularly difficult times and don't press for people to speak if they're uncomfortable doing so.

11. Have you ever made a vow or an oath? Did you keep it? If not, what was the result? Why are vows and oaths to be taken seriously? What role does God play in all of your promises?

12. The role of women in the church is obviously much different today than in Moses' time. Where have you encountered controversy regarding the role of women? How have you responded to that controversy? What do you think Jesus would say about the battles today's church is having over the difference between the way men and women are treated in the church?

13. How do you feel about the violence in the Old Testament stories found in Numbers? How do you reconcile this with the God who loves you today? Has God changed, or have people changed? Explain.

Going Forward

14. Think of one or two things that you have learned that you'd like to work on in the coming week. Remember that this is all about quality, not quantity. It's better to work on one specific area of life and do it well than to work on many and do poorly (or to be so overwhelmed that you simply don't try).

Do you want to better understand why God sometimes chooses dramatic, even violent actions to accomplish His will? Be specific. Go back through Numbers 30—35 and put a star next to the phrase or verse that is most encouraging to you. Consider memorizing this verse.

Real-Life Application Ideas: One of the messages in this section of Numbers is about God's promise to the Israelites. He promised His people the land of Canaan, and (after years of wandering) presented it to them. And yet they still had work to do when they arrived in Canaan. This week, take time to thank God for all the things He's done for you, then take inventory of the work God is still doing in you, and the things He's set before you to accomplish. This could be anything from practical goals to spiritual goals. Perhaps God is calling you to move into a "Canaan" in your work life, or your church life. What are the obstacles you still face in these endeavors? Look for practical ways to address the obstacles so you can continue to live out God's will for your life and receive the inheritance He's promised you.

Seeking Help

15. Write a prayer below (or simply pray one in silence), inviting God to work on your mind and heart in those areas you've noted in the Going Forward section. Be honest about your desires and fears.

Notes for Small Groups:

- *Look for ways to put into practice the things you wrote in the Going Forward section. Talk with other group members about your ideas and commit to being accountable to one another.*
- *During the coming week, ask the Holy Spirit to continue to reveal truth to you from what you've read and studied.*

Summary and Review

Notes for Small Groups: This session is a summary and review of this book. Because of that, it is shorter than the previous lessons. If you are using this in a small-group setting, consider combining this lesson with a time of fellowship or a shared meal.

Before you begin …

- *Pray for the Holy Spirit to reveal truth and wisdom as you go through this lesson.*
- *Briefly review the notes you made in the previous sessions. You will refer back to previous sections throughout this bonus lesson.*

Looking Back

1. Over the past eight lessons, you've examined the book of Numbers. What expectations did you bring to this study? In what ways were those expectations met?

2. What is the most significant personal discovery you've made from this study?

3. What surprised you most about Numbers? What, if anything, troubled you?

Progress Report

4. Take a few moments to review the "Going Forward" sections of the previous lessons. How would you rate your progress for each of the things you chose to work on? What adjustments, if any, do you need to make to continue on the path toward spiritual maturity?

5. In what ways have you grown closer to Christ during this study? Take a moment to celebrate those things. Then think of areas where you feel you still need to grow and note those here. Make plans to revisit this study in a few weeks to review your growing faith.

Things to Pray About

6. Numbers is a book about being counted among God's people. As you reflect on what it means to be counted, think about how to live that truth out in everyday life.

7. The messages in Numbers include trust, forgiveness, discipline, God's provision, and God's promises. Spend time praying for each of these topics.

8. Whether you've been studying this in a small group or on your own, there are many other Christians working through the very same issues you discovered when examining Numbers. Take time to pray for each of them, that God would reveal truth, that the Holy Spirit would guide you, and that each person might grow in spiritual maturity according to God's will.

A Blessing of Encouragement

Studying the Bible is one of the best ways to learn how to be more like Christ. Thanks for taking this step. In closing, let this blessing precede you and follow you into the next week while you continue to marinate in God's Word:

May God light your path to greater understanding as you review the truths found in the book of Numbers and consider how they can help you grow closer to Christ.